Bittersweet Seasons
1947
in
Sussex

GW00497093

also by the same author

The Tree Climbers

(A Childhhood in Wartime Brighton)

Bittersweet Seasons
1947
in
Sussex

with wartime and other excerpts

By
David J. Knowles

Published by
Knowles Publishing
Rochester

3

First published 1999
Knowles Publishing, Rochester

ISBN 09534358 1 4

The front cover photograph – Mermaid Street, Rye.
'In the bleak mid-winter.'
The back cover photograph –
Manhunt on the Downs near Brighton during harvesting 1947
Cover design by Redwood Books

Published by Knowles Publishing
18 Castle Avenue, Rochester, Kent

Printed by Redwood Books. Trowbridge, Wilts.

Dedication

To my wife Pamela for all the hard work.
To Sylvia – for the readings, and for always being there.

Acknowledgements
My thanks to all the following

Michael Ann, for information about the origins and earlier years at Drusilla's, the well known zoo and tearooms in Sussex. Julia Aries, archivist at Glyndebourne, for the story of Glyndebourne, when the evacuees were there during the war years, and for the very special photographs. Chris Carr and Graeme Wright for information and some lines from 'Merrydown – Forty Vintage Years.' Bob Copper for allowing me to use some lines from 'A Song For Every Season' and 'Early to Rise' – books I treasure. Gerald Summers for some lines from 'Lure of the Falcon' – a quite unforgettable book, a must for all animal lovers.

Robert Body, librarian and curator Sussex C.C.C. for information about the cricket in 1947.

Jean Roberts, archivist at St.Mary's Hall and Janet Pennington, archivist at Lancing College for helping me once again, as they did for 'The Tree Climbers.' Brian Green, Hastings Fishing Museum for information about the Hastings fishing industry, and Steve Peak for information and a few lines from his absorbing book 'Fishermen of Hastings.' P.M.of Hastings for her very readable letters. Audrey and Jack O'Neill of Wepham for their enjoyable addition to the book. George B. from near Eastbourne and Reg T. from Horsham for their intriguing letters. Dennis Bird of Shoreham-by-Sea. Philip and Dorothy Robotham of Bexhill for information and photograph. Clifford Bloomfield of Playden, near Rye, for photographs. Peter Kirby for information and photographs of the Ashdown Forest.

Brighton reference library for photostats and photographs. The reference libraries at Chichester, Hastings, Horsham, Tunbridge Wells and Worthing.

Maire McQueeney and Mike Strong from Brighton fishing museum for a lot of detailed information of the Brighton fishing boats and pleasure boats and Brighton Fishing Museum for photographs. Barbara Cornwell of Curd Farm, Barcombe Mills for information of the past history that area and photographs. 'Leave it to Jeaves' Brighton Marina, for photographs. Michael Smith for photographs of Rottingdean and sheep on the downs. John Heron, 'Canal + Image,' Pinewood Studios, for photograph of Brighton seafront during filming of 'Brighton Rock'.

Brighton Evening Argus, West Sussex Gazette, Worthing Herald, Worthing Gazette, Hastings and St.Leonards Observer, Kent and Sussex Courier, Crawley & District Observer. West Sussex County Times. The Times. Ministry of Agriculture, Food & Fisheries. BBC Archives Reading. London Weather Centre. David Turner, for help obtaining photographs. Robert Steyning, for picture of Bishops Palace, Chichester. Ivor Smith for his contribution to the Glyndebourne Interlude. My sons Paul and Tim, for help with the computer work, and finally, my sister Jill for the memories and photographs, and her daughter, my niece Joanna, for the time spent getting me important photostats.

Also my sincere thanks to anyone not mentioned here for their time and much appreciated help.

Contents

Chapters

Illustrations

Bittersweet Seasons
1947
in Sussex

Introduction

My walks over the downs to the small Norman church of St. Wulfran's, which nestles at the foot of the downs at Ovingdean, were familiar journeys filled with many memories. My visits to my mother's grave were never planned – I simply went there when the mood took me and the weather promised that the walk would be a pleasant one. I had made this journey with my mother many times during the long war years, but when she died on that dark November day in 1945, and had been buried at St.Wulfran's, it had afterwards given me a curious sort of inner peace to make the same journeys and imagine she was walking beside me. My actual graveside visits were over in a minute or two, and I would then leave the churchyard and walk back over the downs – my spirits a little uplifted.

1946, had been a strange and unsettled year for my father, my sister, Jill, and me. We still lived in the flat at number thirteen Sussex Square in the Kemptown area of Brighton; my grandparents still owned the house, but had decided to leave there and move to a house in West Worthing, early in 1947. My father was undecided about what he would do when that time came; with a young family to look after, and having lost a leg from wounds sustained at Mons in the First World War, things were tricky for him – to say the least! By the November of 1946, he was finding it increasingly difficult to cope – he had to rely on an army officer's disability pension and some help from a 'well off' relative. He had, however, found out that the plans for my sister's and my own education – made whilst my mother was still alive, could still be kept to, thanks to a special ex-army officer's trust fund, that was in operation at that time and available to certain people who came under a special category, and who because of wounds incurred in battle, were no longer able to follow their careers – thus badly affecting their incomes.

During the first full year of peace, we had seen a lot of our very good friend Sylvia Chalmers, who was now working in London, but quite often visited her family at number forty seven Sussex Square – her older brother, Alec, was my Godfather. By November, 1946, father had asked her to marry him, and she had accepted – undaunted by the fact that she would also be taking on the responsibility of motherhood to Jill and me. The idea was that the marriage would be in April 1947, and that some time after that, during the summer, we would move across the square to a flat at number forty seven.

In Brighton during 1946 work had started on many of the bomb damaged areas, but there was still a lot of 'wartorn' and wartime Brighton in evidence, and would be for many years to come. Most of the static water tanks that had been specially built for fighting fires after the bombings, were still standing, and this included the one in the top gardens in Sussex Square, which had been the source of a lot of entertainment to quite a few of us children during those traumatic years, but never used for fighting an actual fire. I have written quite a bit about some happenings concerning this water tank, in my book 'The Tree Climbers' – a childhood in wartime Brighton; the tank was 'removed' from there in 1946 – leaving chalk all over the place. The top gardens were still open to everyone, and would be until new railings and gates were eventually put up in July 1947, thus, once again making them exclusive to the residents of the square and crescents – as were the bottom gardens. A new lawn was also laid where the water tank had been, at this time. The slopes that lead down to Madeira

Drive eventually became council property and remain open to the general public, to this day. Just beyond this, Volks Electric Railway lay in a state of some disrepair, and both termini had been demolished at the beginning of the war. Eventually, after general repair work on the line and also a new station built at Black Rock, these fascinating small trains started running again on April 15th 1948. Beyond the railway are the beaches, which we could now use again – we did this quite frequently in the summer months – the mines and barbed wire, of course, all gone.

By the end of 1946, there were still many kinds of rationing including meat, dairy produce, sugar and sweets, and allowances for these were to fluctuate considerably during the coming year of 1947 – it seemed the 'quick new dividends' from winning the peace, that we had hoped for, weren't forthcoming. We hoped though, that better things were just around the corner and there was still an air of expectancy alive among the many setbacks we were enduring, and 1947, we believed, promised more for the beginning of a better future.

On being asked, by a Sussex historian, what year I would consider to be the one I would most like to write about – a year I could remember well during my lifetime – the year 1947 immediately sprang to my mind. It was not only a year that was extremely important to me, but also to many others; it was a year packed with bittersweet memories and I have chosen stories and happenings of Brighton and Sussex of a time firmly lodged in my mind and quite simply – unforgettable! I have also included how this year affected other people, with stories and incidents related to me in letters or in person, and, as the period of time I am writing of is so soon after World War II – I have, where I felt it would be apt, included wartime excerpts as well.

Chapter One

Bread units – Blizzards – What do we use for fuel?

During 1946, our small group of friends, who had stuck together during the war years, frequently meeting and playing in the gardens in Sussex Square, in Brighton, had, more or less gone our own ways – with new found friends. We still met up now and again though, perhaps occasionally going to the cinema together, or just meeting up by chance in the gardens, as we'd always done. Mainly though, things were different now and our personal interests and ever changing aims in life had taken varying paths – leading to differing and hopeful new horizons.

One of my new friends, Keith Denyer, lived with his family at number nineteen in the square, Keith was to become a special friend, and in later years, the best man at my wedding. The weather on New Year's eve 1946 in Brighton was mild, with a light southerly wind keeping the temperatures in the upper forties. Keith and I spent that afternoon at the pictures, we saw 'Blue Skies' starring Bing Crosby and Fred Astaire, at the Odeon in West Street. In the evening, accompanied by my father and his future wife, Sylvia Chalmers we went to a party at number nineteen, as guests of Keith's parents, Captain and Mrs. Denyer. It was an enjoyable evening which we spent listening to, and dancing to gramophone records. We also enthusiastically played charades, sometimes seriously acting out our roles, but also with much laughter as well; eventually, after 'toasting' in the New Year, we made our way home. My sister Jill and her boyfriend, had danced the last hours of the old year away at The Regent Dance Hall, to the music of Syd Dean and his orchestra.

On Wednesday the first of January 1947, 'Manny' Shinwell, the minister for fuel and power, announced that the coal industry was to be nationalised – with immediate effect. Miners arriving at the pitheads early that morning had found notices on the gates saying that their places of work were now run by the government and were no longer private companies.

The day before this The Argus had reported that Shinwell had told the cabinet that there would be – "no drastic action taken during the present fuel crisis!" In Brighton and indeed the whole of the country, coal was scarce, with deliveries unpredictable and becoming increasingly infrequent; because of this situation the country was on the alert for even more power cuts, which, we were warned, would get worse before getting better! Amongst many other things, this also affected the rail services. At that time, we still had rationing of course, and although the food situation was improving in some quarters, there was now a disastrous flour situation, with the bakers getting inadequate supplies; most of which was of a low quality – "not fit for pigs" – some said. This situation had first hit crisis level back in 1946 and had made it essential for bread rationing to be introduced – something that hadn't happened throughout the war. This rationing was still in operation, and would be until the end of July 1948. The coupons we used for this were called B.U.'s – Bread Units, and although this guaranteed a certain amount of bread for everyone, it was by no means certain that when you joined one of the long queues at the bakers, that your wait would be a successful one!

At home, we thought that all this was bad enough, but what we didn't know was that just ahead of us were two months of the worst weather of the century, with even more drastic fuel and food cuts, including meat in short supply – not helped in any way by there being a transport strike, with Smithfield Market being hard hit.

16

Indeed things at this time were so bad that it seemed that we were worse off than at any stage during the war!

My father, because of the type of false leg he now had – a stump type of leg – specially made at Roehampton Hospital because the leg had been amputated from so high up, found it very difficult to get about on slippery surfaces, and the winter of 1947 was soon to become no friend to him at all – making him a virtual 'prisoner' of indoors. He no longer drove a car – after leaving the army and before the amputation of his leg through gangrene setting in in 1937 – he had been a representative for a firm of Brighton based builders merchants. He used to travel around the south east of England in a small Morris car he had in those days; he also quite frequently took my mother, my sister and me for enjoyable trips into the Sussex countryside. One of our favourite runs was through the lesser used roads from Brighton to Crawley – an enjoyable run out, which passed through some beautiful countryside, and Crawley, of course, a very different place in those days to now! He'd stop the car at the George Inn, where he and mother would go inside for a drink, and Jill and I would sit outside with a small bottle of ginger beer each; after this we'd have a picnic lunch in the countryside nearby.

On January 10th 1947, father, disappointedly read out from the newspaper that Crawley was to become a new town; there had been talk about this for quite some time, but nothing definite. "There'll be a lot of people still objecting to this!" he said. He had a friend who owned a farm near to Crawley, and wondered how he had received this latest piece of news. Later that day he phoned this friend and was told by him that there had also been a report in the Crawley and District Observer that day, which confirmed that the plan for a new town would go ahead – 'Official' – it said, and went on to say 'Crawley and Three Bridges are to become the Minister of Town and Planning's next satellite town. This is the effect of the announcement made by Mr. Lewis Silken in the London Gazette today. He says that after considering all the

17

objections to the scheme put forward at the public inquiry last November, he has decided to make the Crawley new town (designation) order, 1947.'

"Progress – I suppose!" Father said, "sad – but inevitable!"

When the news had been confirmed that there would be a new town built at Crawley, there had been much speculation as to how this might alter the future of the small airfield at Garwick, so, it was interesting to read the following, which appeared in the Crawley and District Observer:

"The future of Gatwick Airport is not yet decided, but the facilities there, especially the fine approach and the fact that it has been used as a base for charter flying ever since the R.A.F. vacated it last year, obviously suggests that this is a ready made base for the new town," Little could anyone have guessed at the time just what this little airfield would eventually become!

On January 11th, with a school friend of mine, Peter Collier, we went with his mother, to the Pantomime at the Hippodrome where we saw Cinderella; with Ted Ray and Elizabeth French, heading a star studded cast, this was the first pantomime I had seen since January 1945 – when mother had taken Jill, me and some of our friends. A week after this it was back to school, and for me, my last term at Brighton College Junior School. In 1945 the junior school had moved from Bristol House in the main school on the Eastern Road, to across the road; taking over the premises of the empty deaf and dumb school. Before the school had moved, the head master at that time, Mr. Stokes, had died suddenly, and eventually, after the deputy head master, Mr. Burstow, had taken over the helm for a while, the headmasters post was filled by Mr. Bayliss-Smith. On Thursday January 23rd, Mr. Bayliss-Smith accompanied by Mr. Burstow, interrupted our class and asked, "how many of you will be going to the senior school next term?" Mr. Burstow ticked off the names – only two boys said they were going elsewhere – I was one of them. "I'm going to Lancing sir." I said.

18

"You hope!" Mr. Burstow quickly added. This was true; although I had scraped through the Common Entrance examination, I still had an interview to come with Mr. Doherty, the head master at Lancing College at that time, and only then would we know for sure whether I had been accepted and would start there at the beginning of the summer term.

On the same day as this, in the evening, the big winter of 1947 began in earnest. The next day, although there was only a light covering of snow at Preston Park in Brighton, and the biggest of the tufts of grass still showed green on the downs near East Brighton Golf Club, the scene as a whole was of a white and wintry landscape, and the bitterly cold winds quickly froze the snow where it lay. In other parts of Sussex though, particularly in the Crawley and Horsham areas, the snowfalls had been much heavier with drifting, and there were reports of the traffic coming to a stand still in the worst hit places. There were delays on many of the bus routes; one bus in particular, which was travelling from Brighton to Horsham, got stuck on Crab-Tree Hill at Lower Beeding, and the passengers had to get out and push!

During the twenty fourth and twenty fifth of January there were further heavy snowfalls in many places and on January twenty sixth, after even heavier falls, with bitterly cold temperatures, it was reported in The Times that farmers were having to dig sheep out of deep drifts on the south downs, and that east Sussex and Kent had been the worst hit areas in the country. Also during this time, reports started coming in from all over the place of schools having to close down temporarily because of 'no heating and burst pipes'; this included us at Brighton College Junior School, and we suddenly found ourselves on 'holiday' again. Within hours of getting this break from the tedium of the 'essential' math's, Latin and French, several of us, with an assortment of home made sledges, were having a whale of a time tobogganing down the slopes of the downs near East Brighton Golf Club.

At home the electricity cuts were becoming more frequent and also lasting for longer, and the fuel supplies were reported to be at an 'all time low'. My father said at the time, "fortunately we've got enough coal for another two weeks – thanks to always keeping 'topped up' – but what happens when that's gone, I dread to think, especially if things are the same as this – or any worse!" Later that day there were more heavy snowfalls, with many villages in the south east 'cut off' from the outside world, and the few snow ploughs available, were all in very heavy demand! During the twenty eighth of January there were further fierce blizzards throughout the country, particularly in the east, and it was reported that German prisoners of war were out in large numbers clearing up snow drifts in East Anglia and the south east. There were stories of the sea freezing over in places, including at Winchelsea Beach in Sussex , and like the winter of 1940 people were skiing in 'the right kind of snow' on many parts of the Downs; this meant that as you couldn't take more than fifty pounds out of the country at that time, many people intent on going on winter holidays abroad, found themselves better off by staying at home and enjoying themselves just as much – with no money restrictions!

The forecast was for plenty more of the 'arctic' weather to come, but this didn't worry me or my friends at all, we were also having a winter holiday – a most welcome, if unexpected one! Eventually though the cold got even colder and it even started getting to us. The bleakness of it all was headlined in The Argus, with part of the headline saying that 'thousands get no gas!' It also told of people with no heating, and further on in the article it said 'Brighton rail services were disorganized, as frozen points made it impossible to move rolling stock from the sidings.' To say the services were disorganised is putting it very mildly – there was chaos, with many people not getting to work or getting there very late.

In a letter to me from Dennis Bird, later to become the skating correspondent for The Times, but at that time working in Lewes he says "my daily journey to Lewes became a nightmare. Normally it consisted of a fifteen minute trip from Shoreham to Brighton, a few minutes' wait, and then another quarter of an hour to Lewes; but our Southern Railway trains received their electric current from a third rail at ground level, which naturally became covered in ice, so delays were frequent. Sometimes, leaving home at 8.15am I did not get into the office until 11am. I remember another 'minor hazard' – walking up Station Street in Lewes when a whole load of snow fell from a roof on top of us unlucky pedestrians."

The next day, after further heavy snow falls, with temperatures the lowest ever recorded in Sussex, it was reported that at East Grinstead, six foot snow drifts were commonplace, and a woman was seen doing her shopping on skis. Also in East Grinstead, a bread roundsman, still trying to do his round despite the bread crisis, had delivered his load by sledge! Further east and near to the coast, Rye was completely cut off from Hastings, with drifting on Winchelsea Hill and five foot drifts at Fairlight. In The Argus, a nice picture appeared, showing people skating and even playing ice hockey on the pond at Falmer. In a more westerly direction the Worthing Herald reported – 'Both milk and bread supplies for the week-end were threatened yesterday by extensive electricity cuts. Nearly fifty employees were standing idle in the morning at Highfield and Oakland Dairies Ltd. because there was no power for bottling milk.' The article went on to say that half the pupils were away from Worthing schools and that not since February 15th 1929 when nineteen degrees of frost were recorded in Worthing, has the night temperature fallen so low as on Tuesday.

By Saturday February 1st, we still didn't know when we'd be returning to school, but it was hoped by the authorities that it wouldn't be long before things would get going again – I was quite happy with things the way they were! With all this extra time off, and not knowing how long it would last, my friends and I treated each day as a bonus. On one particular day a small group of us decided to take the sledges a bit further on than to our usual place between the golf club and East Brighton Park. We trudged past the large crowd of tobogganers, eventually reaching a part of the Downs near an old, closed up barn, which overlooked the small valley near Roedean School. Beyond this, the sea looked uninvitingly grey. Before we had decided where we were going to try to use the sledges, we were puzzled to see a few snowflakes coming down from a clear blue sky. To be more precise, these flakes were being driven along by a increasing wind. Within minutes what had been a bright day, had now suddenly darkened – literally 'from out of the blue' – and we found ourselves caught out in a ferocious blizzard, with no cover. We couldn't get into the barn, so we filed over to the west side of it, and this did offer us some shelter from the thickening and hard driving snow. "I've never been as cold as this in my life before!" I told the others.

"Nor me!" one of my friends, Peter, said.
A bit later, with the snow easing a bit, we trundled the sledges off the Downs, and hurriedly made our way back towards our homes. On the way, Peter said, "I think I'll give up any ideas I had of becoming an arctic explorer!"

"Why's that?" I asked him.

"Well" – Peter replied "the snow's all very well – but they should make it warmer!"

"Who's they?" I asked.

"Well – God or whoever it is who manages the weather from up there!"

"What – a sort of heavenly central heating angel who can provide ready heated snow?" I said.

"Yes, something like that." he replied. We laughed and carried on our way home – the sledges, for that afternoon, unused.

That evening, Aunt Daphne took Jill and me to the Hippodrome to see Max Miller, it was the first time I had seen him on the stage, but often used to see him, wearing his familiar large trilby hat , walking along the seafront. Father, when attending as an out patient, the army officers hospital that used to be in Percival Terrace, quite often used to see him and speak to him while on his way there or back – "a very nice man to talk to, and quite unassuming. " He once told me.

The following Tuesday, an uncle of mine who had been due to call on us, phoned us to say that he couldn't make it because he was snowed up in Rye. He told father that he'd gone there to see about buying a boat he had seen advertised, and stay for just one night, looking up some old acquaintances while he was there; but overnight snow had meant him staying for longer than he had planned. He said that walking about in Rye was difficult enough, and many country roads were reported to be blocked as well – so motoring through to Brighton at the moment wasn't on the agenda. He also said that he had put up at 'The Mermaid Inn' at Rye and would now enjoy an enforced and unexpected holiday, sitting at the bar enjoying a 'drink or three' and eating like royalty! "I don't mind if it does last." He told father cheerfully.

By February 5th – With the bad weather continuing, there were reports from all over the county, not only of further snow falls but also of rainfall and melting ice causing floods and then freezing again. When the temperatures did relent a bit from time to time and the huge amounts of snow started to melt, the Worthing Gazette reported. ' – Already this month has lived up to it's name of "February fill dyke" – melting snow and driving rain have imposed a burden too heavy for the storm water system to bear. By Sunday evening the Littlehampton Road between Goring Roundabout and Durrington Lane was deep under water and practically impassable and a flood warning was erected on the road by the roundabout. On the main bus route between Worthing and Littlehampton there was further flooding and passengers were treated to the unusual spectacle of 'apparent' waves breaking on either side of the double decker as it splashed through the water.'

The saddest incident of that winter occurred on the sixth of February at Crowborough. Three boys with a dog were exploring the thick undergrowth near New Mill Pond – the pond was still iced over, so the boys started throwing stones onto the ice for the dog to chase; two of the boys followed the dog onto the uncertain surface, despite being warned not to by the third boy. The ice broke and the boys fell into the water. The third boy tried extending a branch he had found nearby to them – without success. William Jarvis of Crowborough Warren, who was working nearby said he heard shouts and took a rope to the waters edge, where he could only see one of the boys but the ice prevented him wading all the way out to the boy. "I then threw the rope over the boys hands, but the rope floated off when I tried to pull." Mr. Jarvis said.

George Ruewell of New Mill Cottages, said that by the time that he arrived Mr. Jarvis was up to his waist in the water. "I ran back to the house and got a ladder and some grappling hooks and tried to rescue this boy – the other one had disappeared. Because of the ice, my efforts were in vain and Mr. Jarvis had to come out of the water because it was so cold." It was not until after seven o'clock that evening that the bodies were recovered; artificial respiration was applied in both cases, but without avail. The fathers of the boys both agreed that it would be a blessing to everybody if the pond could be drained, and Mr. Ruewell observed that there had been deaths there every year during the period he had been in the district!

A report from the Worthing Herald on February 7th under the headlines 'Workers May Be Stood Off'- went on to say, 'Chaotic conditions due to fuel cuts. Laundries and light industries in Worthing which use electrical plant are seriously affected by cuts and the coal shortage. One laundry warns that it may have to close down; another said employees may be given notice. "Delivery is likely to take three weeks or a month," the 'Herald' was told.

Drastic cuts in coal allocations to local laundries have created a condition variously termed "chaotic," "very grim," and a threat to the health of the public!'

On the same day as this we had our worst power cut so far – from 5.30 p.m. to 9.30 p.m. – during which time, people relying on electricity for heating – simply shivered, or as one man has written and told me – "I took my family to our local pub for the evening, children and all, they had a large log fire burning and numerous candles throwing out an adequate and 'cosy' sort of light." He said. "That wasn't the only time either, during those power cuts – I remember we had some enjoyable, if expensive, evenings!" he added. Many pubs used to carry on business by using candles during the crisis, and it soon became difficult in many places to buy these 'lifelines,' which some people even cooked by or simply heated water on.

During the coldest of the weather at that time, at Littlehampton, a train literally froze to the rails! Apparently the warmth of the train, when it had completed it's run from Victoria, had melted the snow on it; this ran down the wheels and froze them to the lines. When the train was eventually 'freed', a railway official said " – and what a noise it made freeing it – like trees crashing to the ground, the entire train was frozen hard to the rails!"

The Chichester correspondent for the West Sussex Gazette, amusingly wrote of the situation of that time in his weekly article:

"Whatever you do, don't write about the snow; we know it is here!" 'Warned a well known Cicesterian, met while skating along the cathedral walk during last week. But such is the widespread circulation of the West Sussex Gazette that Cicesterians abroad will surely wish to see it recorded that Chichester failed to escape the snow and blizzards that swept the south. The pleasure derived by a young son from these arctic conditions, forbids reproduction of a string of comments as one contemplated the rigours while trying to shave and prepare breakfast during cuts in the electricity, or the tremors induced by anticipation of frantic mopping up when the thaw should reveal weaknesses in the household plumbing system. Instead a tribute may be paid to the magnificent way in which public services, in the main, overcame difficulties and helped to reduce the discomforts and trials of the local population. Everywhere there was loud praise for the way in which the bus services functioned in conditions more suited to the Cresta Run. The services to Duncton had to be cancelled, while others to Petersfield were able to go as far as Chilgrove on one road, and Compton on the other, before the snow drifts and ice became impassable. Around the Lavant area there were drifts 6ft. to 8ft. deep and in several areas to the south of the city, transport had to be dug out of the snow before the roads could be opened. Fortunately no serious accidents occurred, though several buses left the road surface into shallow ditches without injury to passengers.'

"Things will have to be pretty bad before we give up". 'Said head postmaster Mr. H.Goldfinch – a remark which typified the determination of the whole of the staff to ensure that the mail went through. Although most of the rounds, including those to outlying farms, were completed on foot, postal deliveries were made without undue dislocation of the schedules.

In the city the surveyors department cleared the main streets on three occasions, only to be faced next morning with a similar task when fresh snow settled inches thick. A large team of sweepers was reinforced by German Prisoners of War; the quality of the labour they contributed was an illustration of typical Teuton thoroughness.

For the rest, the city suffered from current and coal shortages with the rest of the nation; the knowledge that the privations were shared universally did not have a mitigating effect. Instead, one felt that in the twentieth century man can no longer claim to have 'defeated' the elements – and 1947 is most certainly an example of this.'

The effect that the power cuts had on industry was also now worsening, causing much difficulty for factories – Allen West's on the Lewes Road in Brighton had to lay off 500 workers for a while and the next day it was announced that because of the fuel crisis, the royal mint would close down and stay closed until the emergency was over! It was also announced that the prime minister would speak to the nation about the crisis that night on the radio.

On February 11th , a shivering Britain faced even more drastic power cuts with rail and bus services badly affected.

On the fourteenth of February, St.Valentines Day, The Argus headlined – 'Sussex roads a vast skating rink!' Also, by now, there were all sorts of stories going around about hardships endured during that "horrific" winter. There were tales of how people were substituting anything they could that would burn, that they wouldn't miss too much, such as old furniture; anything which might throw out some heat when burnt. There were also reports from towns that used to have trams, that the wooden blocks that held the tracks, that were still there, were being dug up for fuel. These wooden blocks, which were already soaked in tar of course from when the roads were 'tarmacked,' burnt extremely freely and very unpredictably – sometimes exploding and showering the room with burning embers, and also setting light to chimneys. The fire brigades in those areas were kept very busy during the winter of 1947. Digging the roads up, was of course illegal and usually done stealthily at night. Under the circumstances though, the police turned a 'blind eye' whenever possible – they too were suffering in the crisis!

One man, who lived in the country near Horsham at that time, was trudging through the snow along an isolated stretch of road, to get to his local pub, about a mile away from his home; on passing a small wooded area, about halfway on his journey he was amazed to see a woman he recognized as a neighbour of his, staggering out of the wood carrying a large sack over her shoulder – "kindling wood" – she said embarrassingly grinning at him – at that moment her husband and two teenage sons also appeared from the wood; they were carrying small trees on their shoulders – "gotta' burn something". The father said, and they went on their way. A couple of hours later, on his way back from the pub, the man came upon exactly the same thing happening again – the same family suddenly appeared from the wood, but this time the father offered the man the use of his bow saw – this offer he readily accepted and before many more minutes had passed, during which time he had cut down a suitable tree that he felt he felt he could manage to balance on his shoulder and get home, he then – somewhat bemused by it all – found himself the 'tail end Charlie' of a small procession, carrying freshly cut small ash trees on their adequate shoulders, through the bleak midwinter's night – all in order to 'keep the home fires burning'! In his letter to me, the man, who prefers not to be named, went on to say that while they were on their way home that night, carrying their heavy loads, they passed one particularly large house, where, because there was a power cut at the time and they could see the flickering of candlelight coming from one of the windows, "I remember thinking" he said, " that it would have been apt for 'Good King Wenceslaus' to have been looking out on them as they trudged past in the deep snow, '– gathering winter fuel!'

The Polar conditions continued for the rest of February, with no 'long term' signs of any let up. At home things continued in very much the same way; the fuel cuts were drastic and very troublesome, the bread shortage continued – but life carried on. Now and again, if I could afford it, I would go to the pictures – sometimes by myself – sometimes with a friend. I remember on one evening Keith and I went to see David Lean's version of 'Great Expectations' with Johns Mills and Alec Guinness, for the second time – it was back at the Regent cinema 'by public demand' – this brilliant film was first released in 1946.

On 21st February, my Aunt Daphne, having a night off from her own very young children, took Jill and me to the Ice Rink in West Street, where I saw my first ice hockey match, between Brighton Tigers and Wembley Lions. On that night, I sat enthralled, and even carried away from time to time with excitement, as 'The Tigers' beat 'The Lions' by three goals to two in the national ice hockey league. Daphne used to be a professional skater and had appeared in several pre war shows at the ice rink; she knew several of the players and after the game introduced Jill and me to some of them – including Bobby Lee, the captain. I left the rink that night firmly 'addicted' and for several years to come remained a faithful supporter of Bobby Lee and his team of 'Canadian Brightonians'.

Towards the end of February, my Uncle Charles, in his old Austin Saloon, drove my father and me across the old toll bridge that spans the River Adur. We turned off by the Sussex Pad Hotel and took the small private road that leads up to Lancing College. It was the day of my interview with Mr. Doherty, the headmaster. After a brief interview we were on our way home again, and I was now a crisp one pound note the richer – an incentive bonus promised to me by my father if I was successful in getting into Lancing – in other words if I had passed 'muster'! All was now fixed, and for my father, things were beginning to look settled again. Jill, who had attended a course at 'Lucy Clayton's' modelling school in London in 1946 was now beginning a modelling career, and I would start at Lancing at the beginning of the summer term; also, before this, he would marry Sylvia Chalmers – the date being fixed for April 10th, but before what promised to be a constructive and eventful April arrived, we had March to come, and the weather, in its fickle ways, still had some more unexpected cards to play!

Chapter Two

More blizzards – The floods arrive

In Brighton, in the nineteen twenties and thirties, apart from political upheaval, strikes and unemployment, which of course affected the whole of the country, life followed very much the same patterns. There were differing fads and fashions of course, and eventually war would break out, but in the meantime life continued very much in the same vein. In 1926, the author, Graham Greene spent a couple of weeks in Brighton recuperating after an illness, which included having fainting spells, and at first was wrongly diagnosed as being 'Epilepsy.' Although his book 'Brighton Rock' is set in 1938, it is thought that the seeds of an idea for this famous work of his, first came to his mind during that stay in Brighton – a place close to his heart – which he often visited. It was also in 1926 that he first converted to Catholicism, and he later admitted that this eventually 'inspired' him to change the format of the book by writing as a 'Catholic writer.' He did a lot of work on changing the book after the first fifty pages whilst he was in Mexico in 1937, and he said after the book was published, that had he read the first fifty pages again after changing the latter part of the book – he would have changed that as well! Because of this, it was going to be interesting to see what the film version would make of the story.

On February 27th 1947, on the Palace Pier, Richard Attenborough and Carol Marsh were photographed by the local press – 'mapping out' the location shots for the film of the book. Some of the filming was already 'in the can' – but the scenes on the seafront, the Palace Pier, the Racehill and other relevant places, were to be shot during the 'hopefully' better weather to come in the summer months. I don't remember any significance in these facts at that time, but in the months to come, my sister, Jill, would be very much 'caught up' in the making of the film.

On March 1st 1947, with the power cuts now affecting even more of industry, and the coal situation at its 'crisis' worst, it was announced that because it took a ton of coal to make a ton of glass there was now a bottle crisis, and the public were implored to rake out every bottle that they could, and simply take them back to where they got them. My father, who used to buy quart bottles of 'India Pale Ale' from Beeney's the grocers and off-licence in Rock Street, now taken over by Mr. Saunders and his family, said to me, "If you take all the empty quart bottles that there are in the cellar back to the shop, you can keep the money to come back on them."

During the next hour or so I made three journeys down to Beeney's, each time carrying a shopping basket full of empty bottles in each hand; at the end of this invigorating bit of labour, I was pleased to find that I was eleven shillings and eight pence the richer – a useful deed carried out during a crisis – and a profit to go with it!

Later that morning with my new found wealth burning a hole in my pocket, I offered my school friend, Peter Collier, the chance to go fishing at a pond he had told me about, near Ditchling – saying that I would pay the bus fares. We arrived at this tree surrounded stretch of water at just after mid day and despite the bitter cold, settled down for an afternoon's sport. No sooner had we started fishing than there was a sudden snow storm, then a bright spell, then snow again, and so on throughout the time we were there. To keep warm we lit a small fire a few yards away from where we were fishing. About an hour after we had lit this fire, and while we were both standing at the waters edge watching our floats – which we had cast out to where the ice was well

31

broken – Peter suddenly called out to me, "David, just look at that bird by the fire!" I looked over my shoulder and was amazed to see a bedraggled and very cold looking hen pheasant standing no more than four feet from our fire, and about ten yards from where we were standing by the pond. On approaching this stricken bird – which was obviously just trying to get warm – it made no move to get away from me. Eventually, with hardly any struggle on the part of the bird, I was able to pick it up! Within minutes I had told Peter I was going to try and save this creature somehow, and asked him to pack up my fishing gear for me as quickly as possible, while I held on to the bird, which was still offering no resistance to my holding it.

At this stage I had every intention of taking the bird back home with me, however, on our way to the bus stop, we passed a cottage where a man was busy splitting up logs in his garden. He called out to us – "What've you got there then?" – we stopped and I showed him the bird, telling him about finding it by our fire. The man said – "the poor thing looks close to death – but as I've brought other birds back from the brink of death before – I don't mind having a go with this one, if you like?" I was hesitant about this at first, but quickly realised that this would mean that the bird got immediate attention, and agreed to his kind offer. Half an hour later we left the man with the pheasant – but only after I had also left him with my telephone number, and he had promised that he would let me know how the bird got on. Two days later, my father told me that this gentleman had phoned to say that the pheasant was making a surprisingly good recovery – "a survivor!" he had said. Three weeks after this my Uncle Charles drove me to Ditchling where I saw this beautiful bird – now fully recovered. A little later we watched as it was released back into the wild.

It was during the early days of March that we noticed that the frosts seemed to be becoming even more severe, and there was further snow. In the Worthing Herald on March 7th under the headline – 'Chaos On Railway' the article went on to say –

'Blizzards and another freeze-up this week completely dislocated rail traffic between Worthing and London. Trains which left Victoria during the evening pulled into Worthing Central station in the early hours of the morning carrying passengers who had spent much of the night waiting at sidings. One train arrived at 3am yesterday, after a journey of nearly nine hours. Many of the travellers were business people who were able to snatch only a few hours sleep before taking the morning train to London again. On the same day, in The Horsham Times, a report said – 'The freak blizzard which swept across southern England on Tuesday evening wrought havoc with train services in the Crawley district, and home-bound travellers were delayed for many hours.

As the result of ice forming on the conductor rails, electric trains were halted on the Horsham, Crawley and Three Bridges lines, and steam locomotives were used to pull them to their destinations.' The report goes on to say, 'Vivid flashes lit the night sky from electric trains, reminding passengers of the blitz days.'

On Saturday 8th March, on the front page of The Hastings and St.Leonards Observer, under the headline – Amazing scenes in glazed forest, the report then said –

"Heavy rain which set in on Tuesday afternoon in the Hastings district, after the spell of frequent snow storms and almost unbroken frost, produced another surprise from winter's repertoire in the form of a heavy glazed frost, which continued all the week. Although causing picturesque scenes in parks, gardens and woodlands, it resulted in widespread damage to trees, telegraph and telephone lines, and considerable disorganization of road transport." The article went on to say that " – In Alexandra Park and other areas, trees were so thickly glazed that the weight of the ice broke off many of the branches".

For the next few days there was quite a mixture of weather, and by Friday 14th March the flooding and snow falls, if anything, also seemed to be getting worse. According to one headline there were 20,000 square miles of the country flooded, with road and rail chaos as water rise. Steadily rising floods in the south and east, brought further chaos on the roads, with seriously interrupted trains. More villages were cut off, houses and parts of towns marooned, and further thousands of acres of land were inundated, and flood water poured over main roads and railways.

The national newspapers were reporting that there was still plenty of snow about as well as the floods. The Sussex Daily News headlined – 'England Cut In Two By Floods' – then said, 'Snowdrifts and water meet. Already battling against paralysis, threatened by floods or snow, much of Britain last night saw conditions become even more menacing!'

In Dorset the army were using flame throwers to clear the drifts. A hamlet near Widdecombe-in-the-Moor, Devon, sent a telegram saying – "No bread since January 27th – starving!"

Barbara Cornwell, who's family have farmed at Curd Farm, Barcombe Mills, for more than a century, kindly lent me a picture taken in 1947, which shows a farm worker with a horse pulling a cartload of wood for fuel, through a flooded road at Barcombe Mills – the only transport that could get along the roads in that picturesque part of Sussex, not far from Lewes.

The farmers in general were having a really bad time of it. An article in The Kent and Sussex Courier said – "Farmers in Kent and Sussex are faced with the gravest crisis they can remember. Flooding, following six disastrous weeks of snow and frost is likely to delay for several more weeks the 1947 programme, which is already months behind schedule. However, Mr. Grant Currie, of Brighton, one of the chief market gardeners in Sussex said:-

"Although the weather has reduced supplies there will be something for everybody, but prices will be higher." Giving an example of this Mr. Currie said "The housewife who has been used to having 3lbs. of broccoli will now have to content herself with one pound at the price of 3lbs!"

Weighing up the situation, Father said that amongst his group of friends there seemed to be an air of resignation about the whole situation, but that everyone was hoping that the beginning of Spring or the beginning of April, whichever came first, would hopefully bring an end to the nightmare. On the lighter side he told Sylvia and me about drinking his evening 'glass or two of beer' by candlelight. On week-day evenings, at 6.30pm sharp, he would walk round to his 'local' – The Rock Inn in Rock Street – spend an hour talking to his friends over a drink or two, and at 7.30pm sharp, leave off to come home – as someone said – "You could set the clock by him!" He told us that he was quite enjoying drinking beer by candlelight – "It seems to make the conversation more interesting – more atmospheric, and I have to be extra strong willed to come away at my usual time." He said.

Sylvia didn't say anything about his coming home half an hour or so later, the past few evenings.

The pavements were now nearly free of snow, but there were still large piles of it in the gutters. In the gardens there were still patches of snow here and there where it had settled more thickly, and there were also the remains of sturdily built snowmen on some of the lawns.

"It's the severe night frosts that are the trouble," father said, "I have to wait until nearly mid-day before I dare venture out."

Frosts were also playing havoc on roads throughout the county – throughout the 'country' in fact! There were many reports of accidents caused by skidding.

Uncle Charles told us that he had had a lucky escape when his car had suddenly skidded round, and flattened a bus stop near the Devil's Dyke, and I had witnessed a bus descending the small hill to the stop oposite St. Mark's Church – spin around, as if in slow motion – and come to a standstill between the phone boxes and the Kiosk, on the Eastern Road.

With the weather situation becoming even more unpredictable, the bread situation was also getting even worse – with more queues and less bread. This situation continued despite reassurances from various quarters, and was to continue for quite some time. The government were giving out a different story though, and even by just before the Whitsun Holidays they were still saying that the holiday bread situation in coast resorts was safe, but bakers in Brighton and Hove met the Mayor (Cr. H.C. Andrews) to protest against a "desperate situation". There was talk at the meeting of panic over non existent flour stocks, but again the bakers received an assurance that there was no need to worry. The bakers then declined the Mayor's offer to head a deputation to London, it was reported. This was following an SOS from a leading Brighton and Hove baker, who said that if manufacture was continued at the present rate, flour stocks would be exhausted by 1st June. On receiving this information Cr.Andrews wired the food ministry asking for immediate relief – "I am taking this matter very seriously" – said the mayor. "With the great influx of visitors the 5% reduction in your flour allocation will not only deprive resident consumers of their rations, but also deprive visitors of their entitlement!" The mayor added that his information was that there were no stocks in Brighton or Hove! This situation was of course widespread, and with the harshness of the winter, the fuel crisis and general transport disorganization – things at this time were desperate, to say the least!

Many people have written to me about how that winter had affected them. One letter in particular from a lady who had just moved to Hastings at that time, tells a very bleak story. She writes:

"I moved to Hastings in that dreadful winter, into two rooms in the old town. There had been heavy snow falls that had turned into ice. The roads, the paths, the roofs were all covered in what looked like eight or nine inches, thickness of snow. My front window looked out onto the East Hill, and what struck me most was the awesome stillness – nothing moved – every branch and every leaf was frozen solid. The back window gave a superb view of the old town, which may have looked like a winter wonderland, but to me was a winter nightmare! The coal ration was very small, but that was irrelevant as the coal lorries were unable to deliver because of the road conditions; I had an electric fire but power cuts were frequent and I couldn't always afford to feed the meter. Access to the shops was either down a steep ice covered hill – which wasn't sensible as I was in the early stages of pregnancy – or down one of the sets of steps. These were like corrugated ice and I negotiated these by sitting on the top one and edging my way down, one by one!

The food rationing was pretty severe, there wasn't even the consolation of good hot meals, and my diet mainly consisted of porridge made with condensed milk. As I didn't have the use of the bath in the house, baths were taken in the wash house down the road. It was four pence per bath I seem to recall. I still remember the gritty feel of the baths, which although clean were never rinsed properly, so the scouring powder lingered. We were also only allowed 5" of water, and whether it was hot or cold was at the discretion of who ran it for you.

People did their washing in the laundry part of the wash house .

This horrendous winter was followed by a wonderful summer when I had a load of problems including being penniless and nearly homeless; but the winter was a sort of turning point in my life, and I knew if I survived that, I could survive anything and here I am approaching seventy five as proof of that!"

This lady, who only wishes to be referred to as 'MP' has written another letter since then, painting a somewhat different picture of the summer months; some of this appears later in the book.

To some people, the snow and ice brought pleasure – especially those who liked to try their hand at skiing, tobogganing or ice skating. David Wadhams, who now lives in Rye, but at that time lived in Hove, had been demobbed from the Royal Navy three days before the Christmas of 1946. In a letter to me he says that his father had recently got his prewar car, a Wolsey – Hornet, back on the road – it had been laid up since 1940. As a returning serviceman, David had been entitled to 'bonus petrol coupons'. One bitterly cold day during the winter of 1947 he and his brother had borrowed their father's car to get to a place where they might find it possible to skate; finding a small patch of 'blue' on old ordnance survey map, they decided to head for that – Wiston Park, near Steyning. He goes on to say – "It was a Friday and there were virtually no others, people or cars, about. When we arrived there was not a soul to be seen, just this large expanse of white – there had been an overnight dusting of light snow – it was perfectly level and completely untouched, virgin as they say. With much trepidation we ventured tentatively onto the ice and, as there were no ominous cracking sounds, we were sufficiently bold to venture ten or twenty yards from the bank and spent a pleasant hour or so modestly displaying our limited skills before returning to Hove. The next day, Saturday, we decided to repeat the experience, and when we arrived the whole frozen lake was 'packed' with skaters, which made our previous days nervous steps look rather ridiculous – however much fun was had by all."

In Sussex, on March 17th there was a mixture in the weather pattern, with blizzards in some places and heavy rain in others. There was flooding again at Barcombe Mills near Lewes, where the river Ouse had broken its banks, causing much damage to trees – even uprooting some of them. The boat house there, owned by the Brown family, was cut off from everywhere for quite a while. This beautiful, unspoiled and quiet backwater, was where my father used to spend a lot of his time, either fishing or painting, and later that year it was to be the place that my friend Keith and I would choose to go camping at, during the summer holidays.

By the 20th of March things had quietened down a bit and the weather improved just enough to give us the hope that at long last the nightmare winter might be over – even my friends and I were wholeheartedly fed up with the awful conditions, and hoped that March would go out as it was supposed to – 'like a lamb' – seeing it had certainly come in 'like a lion!'

I was now coming to the end of my time at Brighton College Junior School; I had first joined the school in the summer term of

1941. Although I was no academic – I had, thanks to Mr. Bayliss-Smith the headmaster, taken a keen interest in ornithology, and to some extent, this was to help me when I got to Lancing. Mr. Bayliss-Smith was a keen ornithologist himself, and had an excellent collection of photographs. He often gave us enjoyable lantern slide lectures, showing us in good detail most of the species of the British bird population. I found these lectures intriguing, and still remember them well. Mr. Burstow, also still had his lantern slide lectures about places of interest and their archaeology. Amongst the many things that I would miss when leaving the prep school, would be the visits to the 'slightly chaotic' film shows, held by the senior school cinematograph society on Saturday evenings, and also, I would miss the scouts. I was now a patrol leader of 'The Stags' and I would miss the occasional camp fire nights at Hassocks. At Lancing, I would be joining the OTC – soon to become the CCF – 'combined cadet force'. A friend of mine, already attending Lancing, said, "– in the house that you'll be going to – 'Heads House' – joining the scouts is frowned upon, and everyone's expected to join the 'Corps' – as we call it."

On Tuesday 25th March, Mr. Dalton, the chancellor of the exchequer announced in The House of Commons that the Lord Mayor of London was opening a fund for relief of flood damage distress throughout the country – the damage was very widespread. This fund was to gather in momentum, with the government 'kicking it off' by contributing £1,000,000 to it. I remember father saying, "I don't suppose the pound I'm sending will make much difference – but every little helps."

On March 27th, Brighton had a mixture of snow, sleet and rain – the snow, starting off as a blizzard. After this, although the rest of March didn't quite go out as gently as expected, it did at least look as though things were on the change and that perhaps spring was 'just around the corner'. The evenings were staying light until later, and listening to programmes on the radio such as 'Dick Barton' or 'Just William,' now played second fiddle to more adventurous pastimes out of doors. On Friday 28th, father came home, after a drink at his local – The Rock Inn – and informed us that he had drawn two horses in the pub sweep stake on The Grand National. "One," he told us, "is the second favourite – the other one, a complete no hoper called 'Caughoo' – it's 'any price' in the betting!" he added. He told us that he would have a bit each way on each of these horses, as was his system if he drew anything in a sweep-stake, but only a shilling each way on the big outsider, he also told us we could have a shilling each way on our own fancies for the race. On Saturday March 29th an Irish horse which had never run in England before, won the Grand National, it was called 'Caughoo' – this "no hoper" had won at the astonishing odds of 100/1. Not only did father have a 'fiver' to collect for winning the sweep-stake at the Rock Inn, but also another six pounds and five shillings from Mr. Brock who owned a small newspaper shop in Bristol Gardens – just opposite The Clyde Arms; he was also a 'commission agent'. A little later Jill and I were very pleased to receive a ten shilling note each from father's newly gained wealth! The day after this, and before I had had the chance to spend any of this unexpected windfall, Jill made a broad hint about buying some small present for Sylvia and father for their wedding – "a token thought, however small" she said. I decided I would sacrifice some of that months sweet coupons and buy them a box of chocolates – not one of the easiest things to come by in those days – but did eventually manage to buy one, after having a quiet word with Mr. and Mrs. Brown at their shop in Rock Street. The rationing in those days was still quite severe, but fortunately on March 30th it was announced that the ration would go back up again from eight ounces to sixteen ounces per month. The sugar rationing at that time was still just 1lb. per person, per month.

On the last day of the month, I was with Peter in the bottom gardens, we were talking to 'Fryer,' the gardener we had come to know and like during the war years. "Well" he said, "I guess that there's a lot to be done now that all the snow's gone – can you smell spring in the air yet?"

The temperatures had gone up a bit, but although the familiar cold, 'tangy' smell from a mixture of snow and salt air was no longer present, and instead There was the sweet smell of freshness that promised that it wouldn't be too long before nature was expanding into the many varying shades of green that the gardens could be relied upon to provide each year, the winter of 1947, would be one that would be difficult to forget.

The winter of 1947 arrives – Pavilion Gardens, Brighton.

Ford's Green Nutley, in Ashdown Forest, 1947

Digging out a road — Ashdown Forest, 1947

Frozen River Rother, 1947 – Rye in the background

Hastings fishing net shops

Lancing College – A wintry scene

Bishop's Palace Gardens, Chichester

Floodwaters at Barcombe Mills, 1947 –
"The Best Means of Transport"

Chapter Three

Spring at last – The wedding – To become a boarder

During the war years it had been common practice to keep abreast of the news – each bulletin eagerly listened to – particularly the one at nine o'clock in the evenings. At number thirteen, we had an extra incentive in the early years of the war to 'listen in' – as Bruce Belfrage, the news reader, lived in the top flat with his wife and son, Julian. It had seemed odd at times, when there was a night air raid, to have listened to him reading the news to the nation at nine o'clock, and later, find him sheltering with us in the basement, during the bombing. After the war, at home, our enthusiasm for what was going on in the world wasn't quite as keen as it had been, none the less, the main issues of that time, such as the situation in Palestine and the forthcoming partition of India and Pakistan, were still followed very closely – particularly by my father. During March he had received a letter from an old army friend of his, now serving in India, and this had very much revived his interest in what was going on in that country. On the last day of March, the papers had reported that 'Mountbatten had arrived in India – his arrival being marred by violence between the Hindus and Moslems.' One report said that the death toll had reached 147 and villages had been razed and "– vultures feed off the bodies of women and children strewn in the bamboo thickets!" The letter to my father had contained a lot of this sort of news as well, and he said after reading it – "we might think that we're hard done by in this country, what with the bread situation, the rationing and this damned awful weather – but at least, in this country now – the violence of war is over!" To replace his ardent following of the wartime situation, father now kept a very discerning eye on the news from that part of the Asian Continent.

It was at this time that preparations began in full swing for his forthcoming wedding to Sylvia Chalmers, and on the evening of April 3rd, a party was held in their honour at number forty seven Sussex Square – laid on by Sylvia's parents, Dickie and Kathleen Chalmers.

Sylvia's grandmother had bought no. 47 for – it is believed – £2,000 in 1902, she was a widow at the time, and also a very ambitious woman. She and her son, A.G.A. Chalmers (known as Dickie) set up a small school here; it was known as Blenheim House School and was for boys of a delicate nature. There were about ten pupils – they had come from a school at Croyden where Dickie had taught for a while; it was thought that the exhilarating Brighton air would be good for them. Dickie married Kathleen Cave, the daughter of Henry Cave of forty four Sussex Square in 1905. Kathleen, the first born had sadly died at the age of seventeen; Alec was born in 1907 and Sylvia in 1908. One can imagine that with three very young children and ten boarders in the house – things were slightly chaotic! Later on there were two more children – Rex and Mary.

In 1909, Canon Dawson, who at that time was, more or less, given a free hand in running Brighton College, approached Dickie, asking him if he was making any money at the school at no.47. Dickie's brief answer was "no!" – So Canon Dawson invited him to come and teach at the junior school and bring the boys who were attending Blenheim House School with him. This of course meant not only a job for Dickie, but also more pupils for Brighton College Junior School. Dickie taught here until 1914, when the First World War broke out. When the younger masters left to serve their country, he was asked to teach French and German in the senior school. He much preferred this and remained a teacher at Brighton College until 1935. He carried on teaching after this – but on a part time basis. He had given me extra tuition in French to help my passing the common entrance examination before going to Lancing College.

Between the wars, many of the houses in the square were converted into flats, but Sylvia's grandmother refused to have her house interfered with. She died in the early 30's and it was then that Dickie Chalmers set about having the house converted. He and Kathleen kept the ground floor and basement as one flat; the rest of the house was let out into flats. Eventually, in 1947 after my grandparents had sold number thirteen, it was arranged that we would move over to the large basement at no.47 – having the use of the garden there as well. Kathleen and Dickie kept the ground floor flat, and of course, also still had use of the garden.

At the party, which was well attended by many friends from both sides of the families, and held in the ground floor flat lounge, I remember that there was an awkward silence when the new people, at what had been 'Beeney's' the grocers shop in Rock Street, entered the room. My father and Sylvia had both endorsed invitations to various local shopkeepers that they knew and liked, and from whom, during the most austere times of the wartime rationing, they had purchased the necessities of life. Unfortunately, just a few of those present were surprised to see 'tradespeople' coming to the party; this embarrassed me; fortunately though, father, who was deep in conversation with someone at that time, didn't notice anything at all, if he had done, I believe he would have found it difficult to control his feelings. He had often said of the 'working classes' "– they shared the trenches with me in world war one, they ate and slept beside me in those trenches, they got killed beside me – so how can I possibly think that by 'fortune of birth' – I am any better than them." To his dying day, he held a deep contempt for anyone who thought they were better than others – simply because of breeding; a view, I am glad to say I have always shared. This brings to mind a passage from Sussex author – Bob Copper's book – 'Early To Rise', he writes – "our codes and creeds are based on faith and optimism and undismayed by the lack of any suggestion of before birth, we cling eagerly to comforting theories of a life after death. But the period in time, the location and individual circumstances in which we find ourselves first drawing breath, seem to be the results of some hideous lottery – Tinker, Tailor, Soldier, Sailor, Rich man, Poor man, Beggar man, Thief!"

On Monday April 7th, three days before the wedding, it stayed mainly fine and warm all day; there were occasional patches of cloud, but these were swiftly blown over by strong and changeable sea breezes, and although there were quick showers now and then, these were few and far between. I decided to spend a few hours walking and exploring on the downs near Ovingdean and Rottingdean, including walking some of the same paths I used to with my mother during the war years – I simply wanted a 'thinking day' on my own. I had packed myself a cheese sandwich lunch with a small bar of chocolate, a piece of cake and a large bottle of lemonade – all of which I carried in a small knapsack. At just after eleven o'clock I set off on my venture. First of all I walked the familiar path that leads from near East Brighton Golf Club and eventually drops down into Ovingdean, which sits picturesquely at the foot of that coastal sweep of the downs. I passed by Ovingdean Grange, covered in Virginia Creeper – it's appearance still making me imagine 'of ghostly happenings,' just as I had always done when passing this large old house, made famous by the author, William Harrison Ainsworth, in his book 'Ovingdean Grange'. Just after the war, the owners of the house had started serving afternoon teas on the lawn and I noticed someone cleaning around the tables – probably getting ready for that afternoon. I spent a few minutes in the churchyard of St.Wulfran's – placing a small bunch of daffodils on mother's grave, and then headed in a northerly direction, before changing route again – this time going east, so that only the downs surrounded me, apart from an occasional dwelling on the outskirts of Ovingdean and Rottingdean.

I set myself no direct route and simply ambled about, going where my fancy took me. From time to time I stopped to watch a bird – sometimes a blackbird, shrilling loudly from a hedgerow or small bush, sometimes a seagull circling lazily close by, or even a kestrel, hovering expectantly for some unsuspecting prey. Although it was only early April, I still searched for where nests might be being built in the hawthorn bushes scattered here and there over the downs. Even if this had been late in the month or in May, my inclination to 'steal' eggs was now gone – my mother had got her way by simply saying "wouldn't you rather see them turn into birds?" – Profound common sense of course, which, with a little imagination, made it impossible for me to ever even think of disturbing this 'future life' again! I passed by one cottage where I could see that the garden had been freshly dug – ready for sowing – and as I write this, it also brings back to mind a passage from another book by Bob Copper 'A Song For Every Season;'- Bob, born at Rottingdean in a family that has seen life there for centuries, has given me permission to quote a few passages from his works; he writes, "– April saw scenes of great activity in the cottage gardens. When work in the stables or farmyard was done for the day the cottagers, anxious to make full use of the extra hour or so of daylight, went straight on to the garden, even before sitting down to their evening meal. Spades and forks gleamed in the last rays of sunlight and the air was sweet with the smell of newly-turned soil and rich, well-rotted stable manure. The evening would be quiet and still and blue tobacco smoke, spiralling up as the gardener paused to light a well blackened clay, hung in wispy horizontal layers under the lower branches of the budding sycamore, whilst cascading over all from the top-most twig came the liquid, piping notes of the blackbird's evening litany.

A well-ordered, freshly sown kitchen garden proclaims an act of faith. The man that bends his back in April for the practical

53

purposes of setting seeds in the drill is also bowing his head in a prayer of supplication and looking towards the fruits of July and the harvest he hopes to gather."

In the early afternoon, when I felt hungry, I sat on a high part of the downs behind Rottingdean, where I had a panoramic view of the channel, and where when looking in a westerly direction and beyond Shoreham harbour, I could see the outline of Worthing quite clearly. I remembered the old saying that if you could see Worthing clearly from Brighton – it meant rain – but from my high vantage point that day, I felt that this didn't count. Looking in that direction brought my thoughts back to going to Lancing College in the not too distant future. When I had talked about this with my mother some years back, the prospect of going there as a boarder – there were no day boys at Lancing – hadn't worried me at all; but now, I was having some misgivings. I had kept quiet about this when talking to father recently about this new 'adventure' – but now, when thinking about it, my stomach did turn over a bit – 'early butterflies', and I wondered how bad things would be on the day of going there. I sat thinking about this for quite a while, and eventually resolved that I wouldn't let everyone down by kicking up a last minute fuss – I would just grin and bear it, and see what happened!

I finished my lunch, took a large swig from the lemonade bottle, and then slowly descended from the downs into Rottingdean – I had decided that I wouldn't bother about a bus home, but walk back along the flat and easy surface of the undercliff walk to Black Rock. First though, on reaching the pond near The Plough Inn, I stopped and fed the ducks with what remained of my sandwiches, then, on continuing I saw a small shop that was advertising 'Toffee Apples – No coupons required'. I bought myself one, and remembered that mother used also to make the toffee for these each autumn, during the war years. I continued my walk through Rottingdean – the High Street seemed very quiet. Whilst writing this yet another passage comes to mind from 'A Song For Every

Season' – about the High Street during sheep shearing time in days gone by. Bob writes:

"– Rottingdean used to be right in the heart of the sheep country. It was on these hills in the latter part of the eighteenth century that John Ellman of Glynde, near Lewes first started to develop the Southdown breed of sheep so famous." He goes on to say, "– When the shepherds were taking their flocks on to new grazing ground and had to pass through the village to get there, a flood of woolly-backed invaders would come pouring down, threatening to engulf the entire village. The transformation scene that took place would be as sudden as it was complete. The village street, which had been basking in the monasterial calm of a summer afternoon, the only signs of life the mongrels lying sprawled in the scanty shade and the wasps hovering around the fleed-cakes in the window of the baker's shop, would suddenly be flooded with all the animation and bustle of a fair-ground. The High Street would be so solid with sheep that you could have walked on their backs from wall to wall, and cottage and shop doors alike would be hastily slammed. The dogs, in fact, did jump up and run about on the backs of the sheep, urging those in the forward ranks to move along a little faster. With all the bleating and the clonging of sheep-bells, the shouts of the drovers, the barking of their dogs and the trample and scuffling of thousands of hooved feet, the drowsy peace was most effectively shattered. But then, as suddenly as it had come, like a wave that has spent its force on the shore, the upheaval receded, the barking and bleating, the shouting and bustling faded away into the distance and left the street as it had been before it all happened. No, perhaps it is wrong to say the same. The evidence that the sheep had passed that way was liberally strewn over the road-surface and pavements. But this was quickly removed by diligent housewives and children with shovels and buckets, not so much for the cleanliness and hygiene of the street in front of the cottages as for the good of the garden plots behind them."

I continued my journey, going past The White Horse Hotel and down to the undercliff walk. Biting chunks out of my toffee apple, I headed towards Ovingdean Gap and Black Rock – the salt air, strong in my lungs. The tide was well on the way out, and I could just make out the shapes of the old railway rocks, starting to become uncovered. During the last decade of the nineteenth century, Volks Railway had run all the way to Rottingdean – the tracks built on 'stilts' and held in place by what we now call 'the railway rocks'. An old section of the train 'Daddy Long Legs' – as it was affectionately called – can still be seen at Brighton Museum. I then walked through the passageway that had been built adjacent to the back of Black Rock bathing pool, my footsteps echoing back at me, and arrived home well in time for tea.

On Thursday April 10th – the wedding day – the weather was particularly kind to us; it was very warm with a gentle southerly breeze and clear blue skies – "more of summer than of early spring!" Father said. The small ceremony, which took place at Brighton Registry Office, was over quite quickly, and by the time we had assembled in the small garden of number forty seven for some photographs to be taken, it was 'shirt sleeve order' for most of the rest of the day for me. Father and Sylvia had decided to have a two day 'honeymoon' just a few miles away, at Shelley's hotel in Lewes. After we had seen them off, Uncle Charles drove Daphne, Jill and me into West Sussex for an afternoon in the countryside. He stopped the car at the village of Washington, where we had a ramble through some beautiful woodlands, and whilst Daphne and Jill picked some bluebells and primroses, Uncle Charles and I enjoyably explored this pleasant woodland area, whilst deep in conversation. He asked me whether I was nervous about starting as a boarder at Lancing in another three weeks time, but I answered him a bit evasively, and I think he guessed that I might be having some misgivings about all this. He talked to me reassuringly about starting out in life and about new ventures being necessary in the make up of a person's character.

He said "from your track record so far in life, I should say that you should do pretty well – being something of an adventurer, as I know you are!" Later on, while he was driving us back to Brighton after an enjoyable afternoon, I had to admit to myself that 'inwardly' I was feeling somewhat better about things.

Charles dropped us off close to the West Pier, after Daphne had said that she could do with – "A brisk walk around the pier – it'll make a nice change!" We walked all the way round the pier, stopping for a while in the 'penny amusements arcade,' where we had a good laugh playing some of the slot machines, including 'The Haunted House' and 'The Laughing Policeman.' I often went on to the West Pier with friends of mine from Brighton College Junior School and played on these machines. There was something about this pier that was different atmospherically to the Palace Pier – perhaps it was a little more reserved, it was certainly a very beautiful pier – something to be treasured.

That evening, after Daphne had treated us to a meal at a small restaurant she knew near The Lanes, we went to see Anne Shelton heading a good variety cast in a typically enjoyable show at the Hippodrome.

That night seemed a bit lonely at number thirteen, and there were all sorts of thoughts going through my mind. The next morning I decided to catch the bus to Lewes and go for a glass of lemonade at Shelley's Hotel, as I had been invited to do, by father and Sylvia. I arrived just before mid-day, and for about half an hour or so, I sat in the hotel garden – fascinated by the antics of a pair of peacocks that were strutting about 'regally' in their pleasant surroundings. After this I caught the bus to Barcombe Mills and walked to the River Ouse, where I spent an hour or so walking about, without seeing another soul – just looking at nature. The next day, father and Sylvia returned home, and all feelings of 'loneliness' quickly disappeared.

A few days later I went with Sylvia and father to see the film 'The Razors Edge' starring Tyrone Power and Gene Tierney. I remember that this story, by 'Somerset Maugham', of a man seeking to find his inner self, intrigued me very much. Soon after seeing it, I got a copy of the book from Brighton Library, and was pleasantly surprised to find that the film had kept, very much, to the written words. Two days later, the fifteenth of April, would have been my mothers 41st birthday, so, once again I walked over the downs and put a small bunch of flowers on her grave; I knew that this would be my last visit there until the summer holidays. I used to do this secretively, but I was fully aware that things were different now and I was grateful that I now had someone I liked and got on with very well as my stepmother. Sylvia was and is a listener – someone that at that time I desperately needed.

That evening, father listened to the budget broadcast, and said to us afterwards, "they've put the price of twenty cigarettes up from 2/4d to 3/4d – in effect from June 17th – and if that doesn't cause a 'mad rush' in the shops, I don't know what will!" He used to smoke cigarettes and a pipe. I remember that in those days it seemed that nearly all adults smoked – there were no government health warnings then – the only reference to them being bad for your health, coming from the smokers themselves in the colloquialism – "coffin nails!"

On April 20th, my fourteenth birthday, father and I spent a couple of hours fishing from our usual swimming beach directly below Sussex Square – there were no bass about, but we did land three nice flounders – much appreciated for tea that evening. A week later Sylvia spent a complete morning getting my trunk packed with all the essential clothing I would need as a boarder at Lancing, including a very nice navy blue suit for Sunday wear and the familiar grey herring bone jackets for daily use. Whilst we had been buying all these things, at Gorringes, the school outfitters on Buckingham Palace Road, in London, I was told to choose a trilby hat as well – this was very much to my amusement at the time – and also to my friends back at home, when I wore it. I never wore this hat at Lancing and I can't remember any of the other boys wearing one either! I was now all set for this new chapter in my life and memories of the many talks I had had with my mother about going to Lancing, came flooding back to me, and made me determined that no one would notice my 'last minute' nerves – and nervous I most certainly was! If I had been going as a day boy, it would have been different, but Lancing only took boarders. The days before actually starting my first term were spent trying to enjoy my 'last moments' of freedom by cramming as much as I could into them. At the same time, I quietly wished that I could 'just get on with it' – and put the suspense behind me!

Chapter Four

Lancing College – Saints Days – A swim in The Adur

In 1848, The Reverend Nathaniel Woodard, who at that time was already the founder of two schools, those being, St. Mary's Grammar School at Shoreham – a day school for children of 'the middle classes' – and St. Nicolas' Grammar School, also at Shoreham – a boarding school for sons of professional men and gentlemen of limited means, had decided that St. Nicolas School was to be an 'upper crust school' – something on the lines of Winchester. It wasn't until 1858 that St. Mary's and St. Nicolas School, which by now had become as one, was housed at Lancing and eventually called Lancing College. The foundation stone for the now well known and well sited landmark of Lancing College Chapel, was laid in 1868. From then on the college has gained in reputation, with many fine scholars and people in the forefront in many walks of life, proudly being able to say that they were educated there.

In 1940, with war raging on the continent, and the hostilities having got to the pitch that it seemed very possible that the home shores would soon be invaded, Lancing College, like many other schools, decided to evacuate – they spent the war years in Shropshire. Before the college was eventually taken over as a training school for officers by H.M.S. King Alfred, it had for a while been General Montgomery's headquarters. Whilst he was there, Winston Churchill visited the threatened sections of the south coast; in 'The Second World War' he writes – "One of my earliest visits was to the third division commanded by General

Montgomery, an officer whom I had not met before. My wife came with me. The third division was stationed near Brighton; it had been given the highest priority for being re-equipped and had been about to sail for France – when the French resistance ended. General Montgomery's headquarters were at Lancing College, near which he showed me a small exercise of which the central feature was a flanking movement of Bren-Gun carriers, of which he could, at that moment, muster only seven or eight. After this we drove together along the coast road through Shoreham and Hove 'till we came to the familiar Brighton front, of which I had so many schoolboy memories."

There is an amusing 'story' about something that happened when these two leading figures in World War Two had got to know each other better. On the occasions when they had met up, it had come through to Churchill that not only was 'Monty' a brilliant leader, but he was also extremely vain. Quite often on Tuesdays during the war, Churchill would dine with King George V1 at Buckingham Palace; on one of these occasions the two men were discussing Montgomery – " I'm worried about Monty; I think he's after my job." Said Churchill.

"Thank God," answered the king, "I thought he was after mine!"

On May 2nd, Uncle Charles drove father, Sylvia and me on the now familiar journey to North Lancing. During that journey I remembered back to when my mother had first pointed out the school to me and told me she hoped I would go there one day. Her wish had been granted and the day had dawned. We drove up the winding private road to the college and Uncle Charles parked the car near to the chapel. The next few hours went past in something of a haze. There was tea in the housemasters study with the four other new boys and their parents, all present. An hour later I watched as Sylvia, father and Uncle Charles drove down the hill and disappeared from sight. I was conscious of a lump forming in my throat, and gritting my teeth against doing anything stupid, like bursting into tears, and concentrated on what was going on around me. Eventually some of the new boys from the previous term took us in hand and showed us around the school and the sports fields – particularly pointing out 'the grubber,' the Lancing name for the tuck shop, where we could buy various types of refreshments, which were very much restricted however because of the rationing. At six o'clock, the school bell – an inheritance from the wartime days when H.M.S. King Alfred were in residence – tolled out that it was time for chapel. I sat in what was to be my seat for the rest of that term, right at the front – just before the choir stalls; I took in the hugeness of the interior and felt a little awe-struck by the whole proceedings. When the service had finished we returned to Heads House, where, after making sure our personal tuck boxes were all stored correctly in the box room – a place we had easy access to – we went to the dormitory. It is difficult to put into words that first night away from home; the five of us new boys kept mainly quiet, the more senior boys chatted away to one an other, swapping yarns of adventures during the holidays, until eventually it was 'lights out.' Some of the boys slept fitfully, and an occasional stifled sob breaking the silence of our strange new home. I tried to put all thoughts out of my mind – after all tomorrow was another day – I was soon asleep.

The next day, the five of us were interviewed by Mr. Jagger, who was to be our housemaster for just one term. We already knew that the old headmasters house on the chapel quadrangle would next term become the new house – Teme House – making the number of houses in the school up to seven. The name 'Teme' had been chosen in remembrance of the wartime evacuation of the school to Shropshire – not far from the banks of the gently flowing River Teme. In its first term, the strength of the house would be made up from volunteers from the other houses and us five new boys from Heads House, who had automatically got selection for this new venture – making us the first and only set of new boys at the school to start in one house one term and be transferred to another one, the next. Sam Jagger and his wife Pamela were well known in the world of sport – Sam being an excellent squash player and coach, and also a good cricketer, and Pamela, an accomplished tennis player.

On the second day of my first term, I renewed acquaintances with my cousin Jonathon; he had been at Lancing nearly two years by then – he was in a different house, and in the years to come we would only speak to one another occasionally.

At lunch time, I was amazed to see that a friend of mine from Brighton College Junior School was another of the new boy intake that term – this was most unexpected, as the last I had heard was that he was going to Dartmouth Naval College. He was Michael Webb, the son of a well known Rottingdean GP. At 'prep' school we had been on – 'going to tea with' terms. In those days, going to tea with someone seemed to cement a friendship. I remember, during the war years, going to tea with many friends, and despite the rationing, the mother of whoever I was going to tea with would put on something special for the occasion, including a nice cake – much looked forward to! My mother did the same when I had anyone to tea, but I remember one tea in particular that I didn't enjoy at all. I had been invited to a friends house at Wilson's Avenue. Instead of sitting down when it came to tea time, everyone just 'walked about'; we ate bread, smeared with lumpy homemade jam, that I was very suspicious about – no butter or margarine; my cup of tea was without any sugar – there was no lemonade, and what I thought was worst of all, there was no cake – unheard of! I looked forward to making a quick escape, so I could 'replenish' myself back at home. However, I had to wait – the worst was still to come. On finishing our 'tea' – George – my friend, was told to do the washing up, and I was told I could help him! On telling about this to mother when I got back home, adding insult to injury, she said "I hope you remembered to thank them for having you!" – With this she quickly excused herself from the room – probably because she didn't want me to see that she could hardly contain herself for laughter.

On our second evening, there was a paper auction, run by John Lyall, the head of the house, and the house captains. The highest bidder for a particular paper would have that delivered to him in the dining hall at breakfast time throughout the term. There were bids for every national newspaper and some periodicals – I remember I had no opposition when I bid for 'The Ice Hockey World' to be delivered to me once per week.

Our day was made up of classes in the morning, sport on most afternoons – sometimes with more classes as well – chapel at 6pm for half an hour, then two periods of evening school (prep) in the houseroom – one before supper, and one afterwards. After this we had a little time to ourselves before going to bed – the more senior you were, the longer you could stay up. Friday afternoons were devoted to the 'Corps' (combined cadet force) which I would soon join. A minority of boys joined the scouts. On Saturdays, there were classes in the morning; in the afternoons, in the summertime, there was usually a school cricket match, which we could watch if we wanted to, or else we were free to do more or less as we pleased until chapel at six. On Sundays we could do much as we liked, but the services in the chapel in the morning and evening were compulsory. Sometimes we got permission to leave the school to go out with friends or relatives, or if we lived reasonably locally, as I did – even go home.

The first few days seemed to go very slowly, but once into the swing of things we settled into a routine that had its enjoyable moments, as well as its 'downs,' and the time passed purposefully in – more or less – a set pattern. It was a time for making new friends and learning new things; at times there were homesick periods, but these lessened as the term progressed. Not unlike in 'Tom Brown'- one or two of my new associates sometimes felt the need to seek quiet solace in the chapel. On my homesick and 'wanting to be away from it all days,' I found my comfort closer to nature, and used to walk on my own in the nearby Ladywell Valley, an area of great beauty just beside the school and only a quick walk from the chapel. At that time this area was something of a bird sanctuary, and during the summer of 1947, the keenest of the 'budding' ornithologists at the school were treated to a visit from a rare pair of golden orioles, who nested there successfully, thanks to much diligence by quite a few of the boys and two of the masters, in keeping an eye out for would be egg collectors.

There was no half term holiday at Lancing at that time – the only special time we got off, was on certain saints days, when we would be free to do much as we pleased from after the second class of the morning until evening chapel at 6pm. I remember that on my first saints day there, St. Barnabas' day, I took a friend home with me; he was unable to get home – his parents lived in America. He, and the whole of his family had been made prisoners of the Japanese when Singapore had fallen – they had all survived their ordeal. During the years to come I listened to many stories that this friend related about those years of growing up in a concentration camp. On the day I took him home with me, my sister took us to the Odeon in West Street to see the film 'Black Narcissus' – starring Deborah Kerr. Jill, at that time was doing quite a bit of freelance modelling – her picture often appeared in advertisements in local papers, in particular modelling shoes for Sydney Leonard's. I remember that I didn't talk about this at school much, just passed on the information that my sister was a model if the conversation was about our families – as it often was.

On another saints day, a bit later in the term, I took two friends with me to see some of a days cricket at the County Ground at Hove – Sussex were playing Nottinghamshire – an uninspiring match that Nottingham Eventually won. The match that I was really looking forward to, was the one between Middlesex and Sussex, when Dennis Comptom and Bill Edrich would be playing – but that wasn't until the beginning of the summer holidays.

65

On Saturdays and sometimes on weekdays there were school matches. As a new boy and of course a junior, I did manage to get into the junior 'colts' team and on one occasion I remember playing against my old school – Brighton College Junior School and meeting up with several old friends of mine. We cricket enthusiasts at Lancing used to follow the first eleven matches very keenly, and two of their matches from that term particularly stick in my mind – one that I saw and one that I didn't see. In the one that I didn't see, Lancing played away to Tonbridge and were thoroughly trounced; but a name that appeared on the Tonbridge scoresheet was M.C. Cowdrey who scored just 22 on that occasion, but of course went on to greater things! In the match that I did see, which was played on Saturday June 21st, Lancing played Brighton College, and I remember seeing several boys who had been seniors at Brighton College Junior School when I had been very junior, and who were now playing for the senior school first eleven – Lancing won this match. Father and Sylvia came over to watch this match. During the years I was at Lancing they would come over for two matches each term, both for cricket and football, and they always came for sports days in the Lent term, in which I played more of a role. Also on the day of the Brighton match, my sister with a friend of hers, Pat Rose, came to 'see' the game, arriving just a little later than father and Sylvia, and turning many heads when they appeared on the scene; not only were they two highly attractive young ladies, but they were also wearing the 'new look' – long flowing dresses down to ankle length, with waspish waists, created that year by Christian Dior – this fashion coming to light in May or early June. Women, when asked at the time why they liked this look, which was criticised as being irresponsibly frivolous with its figure of eight shape and wasteful because of the amount of material used, answered – quite simply – because they were fed up with drab and austere utility wear! The government very soon encouraged other fashions, using far less material – clothing material of course was still in short supply.

At school, we were encouraged to keep an eye on the news and what was going on in the outside world and at home. In the theatre and music world, "Annie Get Your Gun" had opened to enthusiastic reviews in London – as had 'Oklahoma' at the Theatre Royal, Drury Lane. Everyone seemed to be whistling or singing the tunes from these 'classics.' Also, in June an outsider – 'Pearl Diver' – had won the Derby at 40/1; I remember I had drawn a blank in the Head's House sweepstake for this race, and I later found out that father hadn't fared any better in the one at the Rock Inn. On the twelfth of June it was announced that Laurence Olivier had been knighted, and this brought back memories of just after the war, when the whole of Brighton College Junior School had been taken to see him in Henry V at the Odeon in West Street. Also knighted that day was Malcolm Sargent.

On another saints day I went to visit my grandparents in Worthing where they had moved to a flat in King George V Avenue. They had had no trouble in selling number thirteen Sussex Square – Sylvia and father had arranged to move into a flat at number forty seven a little later in the month.

On Sunday June 22nd, Mr. Jagger my housemaster gave me permission to go home for part of the day. My stepmother had done some teaching earlier in her life, and one of her old students was now at Lancing. Sylvia had contacted him and invited him to come home with me for lunch on this day. David Millyard, who was very religious and would later go into the church, was three years older than me and also had 'red' hair. I don't remember much of any of the conversations with him that day because I was getting used to the fact that the large basement flat at number forty seven – which we had arrived at just before one o'clock – was my new home! Number thirteen – where I had been born and had lived at all my life, was now something of the past, all the familiar old nooks and crannies, of what I knew as home – were now gone for ever! The house still stood in the same place of

67

course, just a stone throw away across the square, but at first I was finding things a bit hard to swallow. I had known it was all going to happen of course, but on that day the realisation of the finality of leaving No.13 – I found difficult to accept. Fortunately, time and the summer holidays would quickly dispel my sad feelings, and this huge basement flat, with the use of the garden there as well, was more spacious than the flat at number thirteen, and after all, I still had Sussex Square gardens, which had become such an important part of my life.

By the time we were sitting on the number ten bus from Pool Valley, back to Lancing in time for evening chapel, I wasn't feeling so bad about things, and with only just over four weeks of term to go before breaking up for the summer holidays – things were even beginning to look quite good! I remember saying to David Millyard that I wished that the present spell of beautiful summer weather would continue right throughout the summer – allowing us to enjoy two months of golden days of holiday – a wish that apart from one 'hiccup' later that month was to be very prophetic! The 'hiccup' in the consistently glorious weather came on Friday June 27th after the hottest night of the month, when the temperatures had remained in the eighties. At just after midday there was a freak violent thunder storm with winds suddenly getting up to sixty miles per hour. This storm, or group of storms, affected most of the south east of England. In London, water streamed through the bomb-battered roof of the Houses of Parliament – through the windows and broad doors in many parts of the buildings, even in the debating chamber, where water cascaded down and splashed the front bench. Houses were struck by lightning in various parts of Sussex – even tearing the roof off one house near Horsham. In just fifteen minutes in Brighton drains became blocked with some streets quickly flooding to a depth of several inches, and in North Street, traffic came to a standstill. At Hastings the lifeboat had to be called out to go to the assistance of a small boat that had completely disappeared off

Eccleston Glen. Several rowing boats were also seen to be in distress off Brighton, and the pleasure boat 'Alexander' with the well known local boat 'Martha Gunn,' towed two of these into the safety of Shoreham Harbour. Nearby, at Lancing College, we witnessed this storm just before going to lunch. In the afternoon the sun shone warmly again and the summer continued as if nothing had happened, except that everything seemed fresher than beforehand.

At Lancing at that time we had an indoor swimming pool – in later years to become the college theatre. This pool was much in demand during that hot summer. If you were a member of the school swimming team – which I was too young to be then – you were allowed to wear swimming trunks, if not, and that included most of the school, you swam in the nude! We thought nothing of this at all, except when – as happened to some of us on one occasion – the parents of a 'would be' new pupil were being shown around the school in general, taking in the pool as they did so. This was highly embarrassing, not only for the mother and daughter of the family, seeing naked youths all over the place, but also us maturing young men who hadn't had time or warning, to quickly grab a towel!

On the last Sunday of the month, after lunch, three of us who had decided to stay close to the school for the day, instead of walking into Steyning or taking the bus into Worthing, decided, at my suggestion, to take a towel each with us and go for a swim in the river Adur nearby – hoping to find somewhere where there wasn't anybody about, making it okay to swim with nothing on. I had told my friends about swimming in the Adur, just below the lower sports fields, during the war years when all the beaches had been closed. I had described how people would come there from Brighton, Worthing and other places in that part of the county on hot summers days, and that the crowds were comparable to Brighton beach on a bank holiday! I took them to the exact spot where we used to picnic, and as there was no-one about – apart from someone fishing about three hundred yards down river from

69

us, near the old toll bridge – we decided to risk having a quick dip. We kept close to the river bank because the tide had turned to go out an hour since, and the currents, particularly mid-stream, could be treacherous. At this moment a family, including mother, father and children walked along the river bank and chose to sit nearby and watch us swimming. As we were waist deep in the water, they were unaware, of course, that we were naked. Also at this moment we were fortunate that a couple of farm hands were trying to get a herd of bullocks from one field to another, which meant their crossing the small road that leads from the Sussex Pad Hotel to Steyning. The family went to watch them, giving us time to dash for our clothes and make ourselves 'decent' again. On the way back to school, in plenty of time for tea, we talked about the holidays that were now only a month away, and although we looked forward to those eagerly awaited long summer days – we had to admit that at school, things weren't so bad after all!

Chapter Five

Heatwave – A Beauty Queen in the family
At last the holidays

On the last day of June the skies remained clear and blue from dawn to dusk and by mid day the temperatures were in the eighties. All along the Sussex coast the resorts were packed and the lesser known 'special' places for bathing, such as Camber Sands in the east of the county and Climping to the west – not far from Littlehampton, also became less isolated than usual, with the picnickers and bathers on those sandy stretches, being a bit more selective in their choice of a place in the sun, in comparison to those who liked to pack themselves 'sardine-fashion' near the piers and close to the town centres. At that time of the year it was a little early for the holidays to start in earnest, but the sun and the sea acted as magnets, and seafront traders were pleased to find that they were doing a roaring trade as early as this – late July and August being their usual 'bread and butter' times of each year.

At Lancing, we too were enjoying what was promising to be an exceptional summer, however in my case I was to miss a few days of the sun. On Tuesday July 1st I made my way to the ante-hall leading to the dining hall, where we always 'stood' and had tea if we wanted it. The college provided a large urn of tea, and bread – we supplied the jam or anything else from our tuck boxes. On that afternoon, feeling a bit sick and decidedly not myself, I scraped what was left of my jar of greengage jam on to a slice of bread – no butter or margarine, and half heartedly chewed at it. I soon found I was feeling even more sick and left the tea hall. A little later – feeling even worse – I reported to the Heads House matron. After having my temperature taken I was told to make my way up to the school sanitarium. Still feeling decidedly under the weather, I walked through the college cloisters, and after walking through the tree lined avenue that led to the sanitarium, I reported to one of the 'san.' Nurses – Miss Derry, the sister of the school chaplain, the Rev. W.R. Derry. I was shown to a single room in the 'san' and a little later was seen by Dr. Crisp, the school doctor. I was kept in isolation in this room for two days and then allowed to join the other patients in the main ward. The reason for this brief isolation was to be made clearer to me later on in the year. Dr. Crisp told me that I was suffering from tonsillitis and that I would have to stay in the sanitarium for a couple more days, even though I was already feeling much better, with a complete return of appetite. In the ward at the time – also suffering from minor ailments – were five other boys from different houses in the school; they were all very senior to me – one of them, Nicholas Browne-Wilkinson – would soon be head of the school. Despite being a junior of the lowest order, I was treated kindly by these boys and included in their conversations – I have always remembered that.

The sun was still shining brightly two days after this when I returned to normal duties. That Friday I was standing on the chapel quadrangle talking to Garde and Sullivan – two of the other new boys in Heads House; we were watching the goldfish in the 'sunken' static water tank, built in case of fires at the beginning of the war, when one of the masters we only knew by sight and by name – Mr. Chamberlin – approached us, introduced himself and told us that the next term he would be our housemaster. At that time he was housemaster of Gibbs House. He told us he would like to get to know us a bit better before we broke up for the holidays and before we all started together in 'Teme House' next term – and accordingly invited us all to go out to tea with him the next Sunday afternoon; we looked forward to this. He had already invited the other two new boys – Field and Goldsack to go out to tea with him on another date; three being the most passengers he could take in his small car.

Sunday duly arrived and we were driven to a small Tudor style restaurant and tea rooms in the country at North Lancing. Despite the rationing, we were treated to toast and jam and two 'home' baked cakes each; we also got to know some more about our future housemaster, whilst he cheerfully and politely appraised us. We had already been told quite a bit about 'Monkey' Chamberlin, as he was nicknamed – more for his mannerisms than for his mildly hirsute appearance. Some of the boys called him 'the Ape' – and these nicknames stayed with him during his long and well remembered time at Lancing, both as pupil and master. We had been told that he was prone to 'black' moods from time to time – but not too often. He was different to the other masters in that he called everyone by their Christian names. He took a very genuine interest in each and every boy, and was a good teacher and athletics coach; he was shy, mainly good humoured and still single at that time. He had been a pupil at the same time as Evelyn Waugh and Tom Driberg. During tea, he told us about Lancing being evacuated to Shropshire during the war and about the River Teme which ran close by where they were evacuated – hence the name of the new house – Teme House. He also told us one amusing story of something that happened while the college was there. "One day" Mr. Chamberlin said, "some American soldiers arrived, and showing a good deal of interest in the school, some of the boys offered to show them around. After a while, one of the Americans, looking a bit puzzled said – 'say – where are the dames?' – they had seen the fancy Gothic letters at the gate – LANCING COLLEGE – and misread it as 'DANCING COLLEGE'! Later that afternoon he drove us back to the college well in time for chapel. In the years to come there would be further outings to tea houses with Mr. Chamberlin, including going to one at Steyning on a few occasions, where, before having tea, we would climb nearby Chanctonbury Ring – "to admire the view and enhance the appetite." He told us.

On July 9th the engagement of Princess Elizabeth and Lieutenant Phillip Mountbatten was officially announced; Elizabeth was twenty one and Phillip twenty six. The announcement came as no surprise, and it was expected that the wedding would be later on that year.

During one of my weekly telephone calls back home in July, father told me that he had had another letter from his friend in India and that he would be coming back home on leave in September and would make a point of calling on us then. From India it had recently been announced that Mr. Jinnah was to become the Governor General of the newly partitioned Pakistan – on August 15th It had originally been thought that this new country would be called 'Hindustan.' There was also news about Mr. Ghandi and his passive resistance – something that would be very much in the news in the next few months.

Another piece of world news – this time concerning the position in Palestine, where the Jewish population was still desperately seeking a state of their own in a section of that country – appeared in the papers on July 18th One paper said – "some five thousand would be Jewish immigrants on the Haganah ship, Exodus reached Haifa today. They used tear gas, smoke bombs, steam jets, iron bars and even tins of food in an effort to fight off a boarding party of British Naval ratings. The fight lasted for an hour and a half, and then the Jews were transferred to three waiting ships. Twenty five Jews were taken to hospital, where three died later. The rest will be taken to Cyprus, bringing the number of Jews detained there to 20,000. The Exodus is an old troopship, previously called 'The President Garfield.' It left Baltimore last February, captained by an American Jew, and with many young Jews amongst the ships crew." The article goes on to say – "The clamour for a Jewish state in Palestine is rising. Last week Dr. Weizmann, the Zionist leader, gave a major speech in which he called upon the British to remove immigration restrictions" – I remember when talking about this crisis with father, he said angrily – "it's about time something positive was done about this situation to help these people who have every right for a country of their own!" But it wouldn't be until next year that the state of Israel was formed.

On the lighter side in the news, on July 15th an article appeared in one of the papers, which made one think of the lengths some people would go to to raise an extra quid or two. There was a scare going on about the safety of potato crops at that time, from being attacked by the Colorado Beetle – some of which had been discovered in this country, causing something of a panic and even leading to there being a notice put in a certain newspaper offering a £10 reward to anyone who discovered one. One enterprising man travelled to France, where he had heard that they could be found without too much difficulty. He returned to this country with four beetles – kept alive in potato leaves. He was caught by customs as he re-entered the country and was subsequently fined £10! His journey wouldn't have earned him anything in any case, because the paper offering the reward had immediately withdrawn the offer after a flood of protesters had pointed out that this would be unlikely to decrease, but increase the Colorado population because of unscrupulous people such as this gentleman – out to make a quick buck!

At breakfast in the college dining hall on Saturday 19th July, I had noticed that I was getting some pointed looks from a few boys on one of the tables, near to the Heads House table. Eventually a house captain at that table, walked over to our table , had a quick word with the head of the house, John Lyall, and then walked down to where I was sitting and said – "Knowles, you live in Brighton don't you?"

"Yes" I replied.

"Do you live at number forty seven Sussex Square?"

"Yes," I replied again, and asked "Why?"

"Have you got a sister called Jill?" he asked.

"Yes." I replied, and again asked "Why?"

"It's alright," he said "there's nothing to worry about – but have you heard from her in the last day or two?"

"No, not for a week or so," and once again asked "why?"

" Well according to one of the newspapers on our table, she was elected as Summer Queen in Brighton last night – didn't you know anything about it?"

"No, not a thing," I truthfully replied, feeling a bit bewildered. With that, he walked back to his table, took the paper away from a group of boys 'devouring' the contents, and brought it over to me – I think it was a copy of that morning's Sussex Daily News. On the front page I saw a picture of my sister in a bathing costume, and sure enough she had won this big beauty contest. In the next hour or so the word quickly spread around the school about this, and almost immediately, boys I had never spoken to before, and plenty of the ones that I had, came up to me and made remarks like – "how about an introduction to your sister Knowles?" – or "Let us know when your sister's coming to see you Knowles – good on you!"

At lunchtime that day I phoned home, father answered, and laughed when he heard that it was me – "you've just won me a bet," he said – "I bet that you'd phone up before the day was out!" He went on to say that although they'd known that Jill was entering the contest – which was held at The Regent Dance Hall – it had still come as a very pleasant surprise when they heard that she had come first, and the phone hadn't stopped ringing all morning – "we are," he said "still trying to catch our breath!" He went on to tell me that after the competition, Jill and the runners up had gone on to a dinner at the Salisbury Hotel where one of the judges – the film actress – 'Greta Gynt' had congratulated her on winning, and had posed for photographs with her. Apparently the panel of judges that had chosen Jill were the entire 'shooting team' of a film being made in the area of Edgar Wallace's novel – 'The Calendar' – and Greta Gynt was the leading lady in the film. Also, Jill and the runners-up had won a trip to see a day's filming on the set of 'Snowbound' at the Shepherds Bush studios. What with all this going on, and with not too many days to go before the school holidays started on July 29th. – I now found the time starting to drag – I just wanted to get home where everything seemed to be happening, and where, in the present heat wave, I could go for a swim from the nearby beaches whenever I felt like one.

On Saturday July 26th – just three days before we broke up – it was another sweltering summers day, and it was forecast by the people who compile the facts and figures of such things, that it would be one of the busiest week-ends on record – with holiday makers already forming long queues for trains to the coast. All the Sussex resorts were as prepared as they could be for the profitable onslaught. One report said that there was a three mile long queue at one station, with people queuing all night to make sure of their place in the sun. There were scenes at some stations that brought back memories of the war – with thousands of people sleeping on them. Most of the boarding houses were already well booked up – but any that weren't knew that there wouldn't be any vacancies before long!

My Uncle Jimmy arrived at number forty seven Sussex Square on that afternoon, seeking a bed for a few nights. When he had been demobbed after serving in The Desert Rats during the war, he, like thousands of other ex-servicemen, had found it hard to settle down to anything specific, and had tried his hand at various jobs in the UK without finding his right vocation – "to be honest" he told father and Sylvia – "I don't know what I want to do!" – He had however just been given a seasonal job as a bathing pool attendant / lifeguard at Black Rock Bathing Pool – just down the road from us. In the basement, the sleeping arrangements had been made for Jill and me to have a small bedroom each, and father and Sylvia the bed sitting room at the front of the flat. They told Jimmy that he could use a couch in the dining room at the back of the flat – that was until he could find somewhere else – this room looked out onto the small garden. Up to this time of course, I hadn't spent a single night under the roof of number forty seven, but now looked forward to doing so even more, as I got on very well with Uncle Jimmy, who was a good friend as well as an uncle.

Also on the 26th July there was a report in the papers that throughout the country an outbreak of 'infantile paralysis' was the worst since 1926, and the numbers were increasing daily – we were to hear a lot more about this dreaded disease in the weeks to come.

The night of the 28/29th July was one I shall never forget; it was extremely hot and sticky in the dormitory and for many of us there was hardly any sleep at all; the excitement of breaking up, especially for us new boys at the end of our long first term, was almost too much. With all the humidity it was hardly surprising that there were a few claps of thunder during the night, but this came to nothing and the dawn broke, clear and warm and still, with the promise of yet another perfect summers day – the longed for holidays were about to begin.

'A gathering at a dew pond on the Downs near Rottingdean

79

After the Wedding, April 1947 – in the garden at 47 Sussex Square
Sylvia, Father, Jill and Me

West Pier 1947.
"A Pier that should be treasured!" – My Father 1947

'The Old Toll Bridge at Shoreham, looking across the River Adur to Lancing College'

Teme House – Lancing College – From the Garden

The launch of the 'Montgomery' 1947
Brighton Pleasure Boat

Blackrock Pool, Brighton, 1947

UNDERCLIFF WALK AND BATHING POOL, ROTTINGDEAN. 1816.

Rottingdean Pool on the Undercliff Walk –
looking towards Saltdean and Telscombe – sadly no longer there!

Jill, having already won the Brighton Summer Queen contest, 1947 – defeats June Pooley (Miss Hove) to become – Miss Brighton and Hove – at Regent Dance Hall. Syd Dean with band in background

Jill, Miss Brighton's Summer Queen –
with runners up Joy Hadden and Mary Bickers on set of film "Snowbound"
Made at Gainsborough Studios – Shephard's Bush.
Dennis Price – Joy Hadden – David MacDonald (Director), Jill, Guy Middleton, Mary Bickers

Filming Brighton Rock on seafront 1947 (Max Miller is amongst crowd watching filming – behind 1st crowd of onlookers – front of 2nd crowd – Tall man, light coloured jacket – hat)

"Queen" and Star

EIGHTEEN-YEARS-OLD JILL KNOWLES, who won the title o: Brighton Summer Queen in the recent contest organised by the *Brighton and Hove Gazette*, shares a cup of tea with Richard Attenborough between racecourse " shots " last·week-end in the filming of " Brighton Rock," in which he plays the part of a " spiv."

Jill sharing cup of tea with Richard Attenborough during filming of
Brighton Rock – Race Hill 1947

A Wartime Interlude at Glyndebourne

There is another story I feel should be added to the book at this point – this time going back to wartime. On the day before we broke up for the summer holidays, a group of us had stood on the chapel quadrangle talking to Mr. Chamberlin. He pointed to a group of people standing not far away from us – just near the chapel entrance. Two of this group of four we knew – one was Jasper Roper the college music master and the other, the school chaplain, the Rev.W.R. Derry. Mr. Chamberlin told us that the other two gentlemen were the composer, Benjamin Britten with his friend and associate, the tenor Peter Pears – an old boy of Lancing. He told us that they were probably discussing the music that Benjamin Britten was writing for next years Lancing College Centenary celebrations. He said that they had been in Sussex in any case for the recent Glyndebourne Festival which had finished two days beforehand. That particular festival had ended with two of Britten operas – 'Albert Herring' and 'The rape of Lucretia,' with a young Kathleen Ferrier playing a memorable Lucretia. In speaking to Julia Aries – the present archivist at Glyndebourne about that year, she also told me of what had happened at Glyndebourne during the war years – when of course there were no operas. The buildings and grounds had been kept very much on the go by the activities of varying numbers of evacuees and those looking after them. She has sent me some notes of those years compiled by M.Fowler and Monica Edwards, who was a resident of Ringmer and a voluntary helper at Glyndebourne nursery school. If I had been in possession of these facts when I was writing 'The Tree Climbers' a story of childhood in Brighton and Sussex during the war years – I would have included them in that book – however as '1947' is a lot about people getting back to normal times just after the war, and as the Glyndebourne Opera Seasons were doing just that, I feel I should include what happened at these famous buildings in the heart of the Sussex countryside, as 'a wartime interlude'.

M. Fowler writes, 'In 1938 with war clouds looming on the continent, the Glyndebourne estate office – without any prior consultation – was advised that preparation should be made for the immediate reception at Glyndebourne of 200 school children – evacuees! Two days of frantic preparation, including filling sacks with straw, to be used as temporary mattresses, followed.

However things weren't needed, Mr. Chamberlain had arrived back in the country, waving that famous piece of paper and proclaiming those even more famous words – "peace in our time!" Because of all this Mr. Christie the founder and owner of Glyndebourne, had given instructions to Mr. W.E. Edwards to act on his behalf in consultations with the LCC – with the understanding that Glyndebourne would offer accommodation in the opera dining halls and other out buildings for nursery-school aged children (babies not envisaged). With the radio announcement in August 1939 of the government evacuation scheme being put into operation, Mr. Christie's London office staff, then mostly scattered on holiday, foregathered as arranged at Glyndebourne, while the small nucleus still in London, hastily packed up the contents of the office for a transfer to Sussex.

Mary Allen, the youngest and newest of Mr. Christie's London office staff and sole occupant of the Cockspur Street office, at the end of August when war seemed imminent, remembers Mr. Edwards telephoning her and telling her to pack up such items as she could and come down to Glyndebourne bringing the money and the keys. Mary remembers seeing vans piled high with furniture etc. She was met at

Lewes station by Arthur Howell ,one of Mr. Christie's Ringmer Motor Works staff. She was welcomed and comfortably settled in at Glyndebourne by Mrs. Daniels, the housekeeper.

All Mr. Christie's staff were brought in on some particular job: one on catering, another arranging sleeping accommodation for nursery staff. Mary was put at the disposal of the nurseries and remembers writing to a dozen or more parents. All took turns at nightly blackout and fire watching duties.

Later Mrs. Young's Chauffeur (a Glynde resident) drove Mary back to London to collect her personal belongings.

On September 1st a mercifully brilliant summer sun bathed the countryside on that morning as the front lawn at Glyndebourne gradually became covered with crawling babies and toddlers, as bus upon bus of London Passenger Transport disgorged its load. The children came from 5 different places – 2 day nurseries, 1 privately run babies home, a large LCC institution for babies mainly of unmarried mothers, and the nursery school attached to the Union of Girls' Schools settlement at Peckham, each unit with its own Matron or Superintendent and assistant staff, and some LCC domestic staff.. Within the course of a couple of hours the Glyndebourne population had been increased by 372 – 300 children and 72 adults!

There is little point in lingering over the difficulties of those first few weeks; all evacuation schemes experienced similar teething troubles. Glyndebourne was greatly blessed by being able to call on Mr. Moores the village grocer for immediate food, and Gote Farm for milk. The old LCC cook managed to cope for this large number on totally inadequate stoves, and the nursery staff cared as best they could with make-do apparatus. Mr. Christie's office staff found themselves doing the most unexpected jobs, not least Rudolf Bing who was seen emerging from a Lewes store with a pile of children's chamber pots! Several of the nurseries had come anticipating that equipment would be awaiting them. Jock, the stage foreman, continued as a tower of strength throughout the nursery occupation. Teenage children from surrounding families (two on horseback I remember) converged on Glyndebourne and gave invaluable voluntary help. A Glynde resident put her large car and chauffeur at the disposal of the nursery.

On 3rd September at 11am the staff gathered in the front hall to hear on the radio the declaration of war – in Mr. Bing's words "a piece of history being made".

At this stage it would be apt to include notes made by Monica Edwards a resident of Ringmer and a voluntary helper at Glyndebourne nursery school.

'Preceding 3rd September there were those two days of intense activity; I remember the round of paliasse filling with straw from the farms and, later, as the babies arrived in bus-loads with little equipment, the long slog of fitting together the 5 – piece, heavy iron cots that had been dismantled in haste with very mixed results.

The immediate need for black-out screens for all windows gave rise to a background of hammering as estate carpenters dealt with this problem – not yet aware that both they and the 'boys' who helped so willingly would soon change their skills to using guns and flying planes. Arthur Howell (Motor Works staff) remembers being sent up to Glyndebourne to 'blue' every light bulb.

Countless messages to help in the early organisation of staff and volunteers to do with accommodation and meals; journeys and meetings re fire-fighting, were relayed from the main office by a few of the young people who already knew the geography of Glyndebourne fairly well. Both boys and girls helped with feeding and care of the babies, as the nurseries lacked their full complement of staff, while some remained in London to pack equipment and to receive still more babies for evacuation.

With the 3rd September announcement no one knew what it would mean or what would happen. Out of doors in the warm sunshine that morning I caught a glimpse of Mrs. Bing in her soft grey dress, hovering moth-like round the curtained cots set out under the trees, she rocked them gently as she moved among them and watched over the tiniest of the babies, thus releasing a nurse for the continuously demanding round of feeds. There were twice daily nappie changes for 300 visiting babies – and Glyndebourne residents came to the rescue here.

Also – and sadly reflecting the bewilderment and fear of some mothers, or single fathers – there were a few babies who had been left in hope and faith on nursery doorsteps, labelled or not, but each in desperate need of care and safety. Two of us in the late twilight of that evening went from cot to cot searching the tiny marked wristlets for the word 'unknown'. I will add some more of Monica Edward's words later.

Continuing M.Fowler's account, he goes on to say – 'Within days it was clear that the number of children was far too great to be accommodated for any length of time and that in any case the out buildings were not suitable for winter accommodation for very young children. Accordingly, the LCC took steps to remove all the babies to reduce the number to a unit of 100 nursery school aged children (2–5), with approximately 35 staff, and the Glyndebourne House itself, with the exception of the wing retained for private use, was handed over to the LCC. From then until 1946 (the children remained after the actual cessation of hostilities) there was a gradual intake of fresh children from South of the Thames to fill places left by children who were billeted in the village or returned home at the age of five.

The members of the Glyndebourne and LCC staffs worked happily together and each will have her own memories, both light-hearted and grim; skating on the frozen ponds in the hard winter of 1940, the long unwelcome periods of night duty, both in the nursery and outside fire watching; making jam for Glynde Church Harvest Festival or collecting sack loads of conkers for the war effort (though I was never clear what Macleans did with the conkers – toothpaste or ammunition?); supplementing the rations by combing the hedgerows for rose-hips, blackberries or elderberries; preserving of fruit and salting of beans; the weekly visit to the village post office to pay in the regular national savings, augmented by periodic marathon efforts in response to special appeals for "War Weapons" or "Wings for Victory" weeks. (In connection with one of these, a very high class auction sale was held under the skilled hammer of Leslie Turner before he left the Estate Office for the RAF). Fire drills and descents by Davy apparatus; evening cycle rides in the country lanes in Summer, completed by a shandy in the village pub; country dancing and the periodic grand dance in winter when the Canadians were stationed on our doorstep – the army and the young nursery staff were not an easy controllable combination! – and the preparation for Christmas and the long awaited day: the opening of stockings, singing carols, tea parties and Christmas trees, and at last, with the children finally asleep, the staff sitting down to a splendid Christmas dinner, followed by traditional party games. Seven Christmases came and went, the most memorable perhaps following Mrs. Christie's and the children's return from Canada, when the party was held in the Organ Room decorated in pre-war fashion with holly and ivy around a crackling log fire.

The translation from opera to nursery school occupation – and back again – was rather amusingly portrayed by finding small children sleeping in rooms labelled "Willi Domgraf Fassbaender" etc. or later, by an opera star, looked down upon by Little Miss Muffet or the Pied Piper, so skillfully executed by some of the nursery school staff on the dressing room walls. In spite of many difficulties, these years gave Glyndebourne the opportunity to make its own contribution to the demands of war and were a continuation in war conditions of the opportunity afforded to London children to enjoy the beauties of the country, already begun by Mrs. Christie in 1938, when through the Children's Country Holiday Fund twenty five children from Bethnal Green were housed in the Waiters Dormitory for a fortnights holiday. It was with heartfelt thanks that, despite high explosives, fire and V bombs in the vicinity, the long war years came to an end without loss of life by enemy action to any children entrusted to Glyndebourne and VJ Day was suitably celebrated by the children "beating the bounds" and waving aloft streamers of red, white and blue.'

Lastly, Monica Edwards concluded her writings as follows.

'A personal memory – of when the spacious lawns were hayfields and a joy to the children, and how they played and wandered in the surrounding meadows, white sun hats visible above the buttercups- also of endless happy afternoons in the coppiced woodland among the flowers and trees throughout the year, their games of 'house' and 'family', their scolding voices and their laughter and their funny confidences. And then for us, if we so wanted, the late informal evenings of listening with Ruddi Bing to opera recorded at Glyndebourne in other years – what a privilege it was.'

One other piece about Glyndebourne, comes from my barber, Ivor Smith. One day while I was having my hair cut, he told me he had been an evacuee there, so I asked him to jot down any memories from that time. He writes –

– 'I was evacuated to Glyndebourne in 1940 – at the age of four. The family had moved from London to avoid the blitz, and we went to stay with a couple of elderly ladies at Preston Drove, in Brighton. They became disenchanted with my tying cotton to door handles – with the other end tied to ornaments and vases, which smashed to the floor when doors were opened or closed; so, only being four years of age, I thought being evacuated was my punishment!

I never settled, and would nightly roam the opera house as I found it difficult to sleep in the changing rooms, which were used as dormitories. During the day I would hide in the beautiful gardens of the opera house when we were taken for walks, and I think that when I finally persuaded my father to take me back to Brighton, everybody there was very much relieved. It never occurred to me that people had better things to do than organize search parties for a child who was continuously trying to lose himself. That was the longest three months of my life.

I soon settled down once I was reunited with my family. I would never make excuses for my behaviour, but would suggest that there is no accounting for the effects of war on young and old alike. Needless to say – I avoided cotton reels from then on!'

Evacuees at Glyndebourne – "'Lovely Summer!'"

Evacuees at Glyndebourne – "Keeping busy in cooler weather"

Chapter Six

Summer holidays – A new home – Film stars
Brighton Rock

I arrived at the basement flat of number forty seven Sussex Square, my new home, at just after ten a.m. on what promised to be another hot summer's day; there was no breeze at all. After the welcoming home preliminaries were over, I unpacked my suitcase in my new bedroom and explored the large basement more thoroughly than I had done on my other visit a few weeks back. In the heat of the day the basement was refreshingly cool. There was a fairly spacious dining room at the back of the flat, which I also used as a sitting room – I was pleased to see there was a piano there. This room looked out onto the garden which I also explored; I noticed that father had already been busy planting out there. There was a high wall at the back of the garden, where there was a wooden door which led out to Arundel Place – there was just one large key for this, we shared this as well. After this I walked around Sussex Square gardens for a while, re-acquainting myself with some of my favourite places in both the top and bottom gardens – even climbing my favourite fir tree in the top gardens. My friends and I had made a secret hiding place in this tree in our younger years during the war. In those top gardens the lawn area, where a static water tank had been in case of fires caused by the bombings, had just been re-turfed, and the gardens were now surrounded by chestnut palings with new gates placed in the same four places as they used to be – this made the gardens, once again, only open to key holders. The bottom gardens, had had this type of palings for quite some time; even during the war these gardens had been for key holders only – Chain link fencing would soon replace the wire netting that had been there since the early war days. During July, Brighton Corporation had passed a resolution saying that they wished to purchase the whole of the slopes, which lay below the main coastal road and had always been a continuation of the gardens and were also for key holders only. There is a tunnel that runs under the road between the bottom gardens and the upper terrace before the slopes; the council said they wished to purchase this terrace as well. In time both the upper terrace and the slopes became council property, and remain open to the public to this day, but you still have to have a key if you wish to use the tunnel.

I returned home after this quick journey of nostalgia, and with an hour to go before lunch I walked down to our usual bathing beach, just below the square, for a swim – the sea was flat and calm with hardly a ripple to be seen. I noticed that the beaches nearer to the Palace Pier were very crowded, but there were just small groups of people here and there on the beach that I was on. I swam out beyond the breakwater on the left side of the beach, on which there were a few people fishing; I floated on my back for a while, then swam to the shore, dressed and returned home to lunch. As I walked home I contemplated what I was going to do until I returned to school on September 19th – fifty two gloriously free days – it was a good feeling and fun to start making plans. I spent most of that afternoon swimming and lazing on the beach, this time I had chosen a beach just beside the Banjo Groyne where I hoped I might see someone I knew, but I realised it would be another day or so before most other schools broke up – however I knew that if the good weather held I would find no shortage of friends and acquaintances scattered about on nearby beaches in the weeks to come.

As I walked home again I noticed that there was work going on on the line of Volkes Electric Railway – but the trains wouldn't start running again until the following year. Later on Uncle Jimmy came home from his job as bathing pool attendant and lifeguard at Black Rock Bathing Pool. He told us that he wouldn't be needing a bed any longer as he'd been offered the share of a flat with an old acquaintance of his he had met at the pool. I was disappointed about this, but knew that I could see him any time I wanted during the holidays, at the pool. Jill also made a quick appearance and told me briefly of her beauty queen happenings and 'adventures', but it wouldn't be until the next day that I would learn a lot more of all that was going on in what promised to be an exciting and eventful summer.

The 30th July seemed hotter than ever, and in the afternoon Jill accompanied me to the beach for a swim – father and Sylvia preferring to sit in the shade under a tree in the bottom gardens. Jill turned quite a few heads when we arrived on the beach, and people we knew slightly from the square and the crescents, came over and talked to us from time to time – usually just to say how pleased they were about Jill's success. While we were on the beach, Jill told me about the 'walk on' part she'd got in the film Brighton Rock and the crowd scenes she was appearing in on certain days. She talked about the film stars that she'd met, including Richard Attenborough and Hermione Baddely. I told her that I intended to watch some of the filming in the days to come – but more about 'Brighton Rock' a bit later on.

The next day, the last day of July, with the glorious weather continuing, there was something in the papers that was to cast something of a shadow over everyone's summer holidays, and indeed the nation as a whole. The report in the paper we took each day said that there were many more cases of infantile paralysis up and down the country – with some fatalities. People were asked not to panic and use common sense in taking precautions against this deadly disease. I remember father reading out that the sort of places that the infection might spread more easily from, were places such as cinemas or swimming pools – in other words places where crowds gathered. This of course began to take its toll on the business being done at The Black Rock Bathing Pool – which is to mention just one place! It didn't stop me however from going to the Odeon, Kemptown cinema that night to see James Stewart in 'It's A Wonderful Life', nor did it stop me from joining the packed crowds at an important cricket match at the Hove County ground a couple of days later.

I feel it is important at this stage of the book to include something about the Ashdown Forest – a beautiful area in Sussex that during the war years had been taken over by the military as, amongst other things, a training area. I can still just about remember going on family excursions to various parts of the forest for picnics, in pre-war days. I can remember my mother saying how much she enjoyed 'absorbing' the views, and can also remember seeing the animals there, including the deer for which we would quite often stop the car as they crossed the small roads – seemingly, with no fear of us mortals. What we didn't know in 1947 was that the military were trying their hardest to make the whole of the area their own! This of course would have 'ruined' the forest and although people would still have had the right to go there the whole place would be a very different one to the forest we know today.

In The Kent and Sussex Courier on August 1st 1947 under the headline – 'ASHDOWN FOREST IS POOR MANS SCOTLAND' – says witness at inquiry – the article goes on to say:

"Members of the public who crowded the council chamber at the Uckfield Rural District offices at Crowborough on Friday to listen to War Office proposals to use Ashdown Forest as a military training ground, heard General Sir Reginald Hildyard, of Hartfield, describe the forest as "the poor man's Scotland." They applauded loudly when he told a war office spokesman: "because you infringe the forest in wartime you think you can do it in peace."

Sir Frank Willshire, appointed by the Ministry of Town and Country Planning, conducted the inquiry and heard many and varied objections to the proposals.

General Sir Reginald Denning, in presenting the case for the army, explained that extensive areas were needed for training. The overall object was to have the army prepared to perform any task with which it might be confronted. The actual requirements of the army were general training rights over about 6,000 acres of the forest, the acquisition of the 900 acre Pippinford Park Estate, and the retention of the camp sites at Crowborough and Maresfield.

"The army will do everything possible to avoid inconveniencing the commoners and the general public," continued General Denning. "We will not fire there or dig. We will not use vehicles, except on existing tracks or roads." The general public would not be excluded from the area even during military exercises.

General R.S. Clarke M.P. for the division who represented the East Sussex County Council, asked whether the whole of the small arms range would be contained in the Pippinford Estate. General Denning replied that a small area to the north of the estate would have to be included.

Mr. J.H. Griffin, representing East Grinstead Urban Council, remarked that many of the tracks across the forest had been made by the military, and asked whether only the roads were to be used by military vehicles. General Denning said that both roads and tracks were to be used in order to avoid movements on the common land.

The clerk to the conservators, Mr. R.W. Fovargue, referred to a meeting at the Ministry of Town and Country Planning in December, as a result of which it had been stated that no vehicles were to be used in the forest. General Denning replied that he had no note of the matter, and that this would not meet with army requirements. Replying to another question regarding safety precautions, he said that the army was covered at all of their ranges by manuals of instructions. Later he said that only blank ammunition would be used outside the range, although they would like to use flares and smoke bombs.

Ashdown Forest was described as 'The Poor mans Scotland' by General Sir Reginald Hildyard, who referring to General Denning, also said, "he comes here from London with its noise and clatter, to the forest with its beauty." General Denning said that the army had tried for months to find a range elsewhere. Amid applause General Hildyard replied: "I am quite certain that if you were told you could not have it you would soon find another place."

General Denning: "We are pushed from pillar to post. What are we to do?"

General Hildyard: "For 400 years no one had been allowed to infringe the forest. Simply because you could do it in wartime you think you can do it in peacetime, and I think you should be stopped!" The article goes on with many people voicing their objections to turning this beautiful forest into a place for army manoeuvres and General Hildyard ending up by saying that not only would the forest be ruined but – "it would be a pity if our beautiful hotels at Crowborough were turned into N.A.A.F.I. canteens!"

The eventual outcome of all this was that the forest escaped becoming a permanent reminder of war, even though the army did obtain several hundred acres of Pippinford Park from the owner, Mr. Hayley-Morris – a reasonable compromise considering what could have happened, and a reprieve for the forest and its creatures and all the people who through the years since then have enjoyed this natural part of our heritage.

On Saturday 2nd.August, I took a friend of mine, Michael, to the cricket match at the Hove County ground to see Sussex play Middlesex – it was James Langridge's benefit match. Father had no difficulty getting tickets for this sell-out match, it helped being the nephew of 'Lance Knowles' who had been secretary of Sussex C.C.C. from 1922 – 1943 and had also played as an amateur for both Kent and Sussex – he had died in 1943. Father was having a lot of trouble with the 'stump' of his missing leg, and decided he didn't want to be a part of a large crowd – so I got the tickets.

The match, which was something of a needle match between these two teams, started disastrously for Sussex; on the first day we saw them bowled out for 145. After this though we were treated to some unforgettable batting by Middlesex in their first innings – with Robertson making 106 – Bill Edrich 76 and Dennis Compton not out 100, with the team declaring at 401 for four wickets. Michael and I went to all three days of this match. In their second innings Sussex made a bit of a revival, with Charlie Oaks – who had been a groundsman at the Horsham ground – scoring 89, and the captain of Sussex – 'Hugh Bartlett' contributing 95. In their second innings though, Middelsex wrapped things up and won by nine wickets, with Bill Edrich showing a sportingly resigned crowd an unbeaten score of 54 from a bat that seemed to work like a magic wand in sending balls to the boundary – effortlessly and gracefully! The Sussex crowd were in two minds – whether it was better to stay and watch this good sport and the defeat of their team or succumb to the stormy rain which had sent the players off the field on a couple of occasions and which threatened to wash out the final day's play with the match thus ending in a draw. This was not to be however and even though Sussex did lose the match, everyone had enjoyed practically three full days of top class cricket.

A lot has been written about that golden summer of cricket in 1947. Dennis Compton and Bill Edrich wrote quite a bit about it in their book 'Cricket and all That' and John Arlott was so inspired by it all at the time that he wrote his well known book – 'Vintage Summer 1947'. One other thing about that match which I told father about when I got home; I had noticed sitting in the crowd in the pavilion the film star Sir C.Aubrey-Smith – one of father's favourite film stars of the thirties and the forties. He was now based in Hollywood but had come over – "to enjoy the cricket" – he told reporters. He was responsible for introducing cricket to Hollywood – with some success. I remember going to the pictures with father and seeing him in the film – 'The Four Feathers' –

106

which we both enjoyed very much. Another actor who lived in Brighton for a time was also in that film – the star of the film in fact – 'John Clements'.

On 5th, 6th and 7th of August, Brighton races enjoyed three days of glorious sunshine and although the temperatures were high – on the race hill there was a refreshing breeze. This holiday summer meeting attracted huge crowds, but quite a lot of the people went expecting to see filming going on for the film 'Brighton Rock'. 'Shooting' was going on in various parts of Brighton at that time – including the seafront, the Palace Pier and the race course where some of Graham Greene's famous book tells of a clash between race course gangs and the ensuing violence. As it turned out anyone hoping to see any of this taking place whilst the racing was going on, were to be disappointed. Jill, as Summer Queen of Brighton had been the first person to sign on as an extra for this film – when nearly 500 people had queued up for parts as extras at the Princes Ballroom. They were told they would be needed for three or four days at £1-7s per day – this was mainly for the racehill scenes, but Jill got other work on the film as well. Everyone was told to report to the racehill by nine o'clock on certain days. There was some controversy whilst they were filming here, when cameramen and crew were 'booted' off the race course. Apparently the time they had been allowed on the race course by the council had expired – or perhaps not even applied for. It all turned out to be a bit of an embarrassment for all parties concerned, but eventually an agreement was reached with the makers of the film – 'Charter Film Productions Limited' being given permission to film on the course from 9th-16th August. Some of the filming on the race course was already 'in the can' and would eventually be used.

Jill told me that she very much enjoyed those days on the racehill, she was even pictured sharing a cup of tea with the star of the film – Richard Attenborough, who plays 'Pinkie'- the leading part in the film – and this picture appeared in The

107

Brighton and Hove Gazette. During the early part of my holiday I did see a bit of the filming going on near to the pier. In one of the scenes I saw being filmed, the camera lingers for a while on two girls looking at photographs on a kiosk window by the pier, as Carol Marsh, playing the part of Rose the waitress, draws Pinkie's attention to them for some reason. The two girls were Jill and another extra called Pamela Baker. Jill got to know most of the stars in the film – She met William Hartnell only once during the filming – in later years, in the late fifties, I would sometimes catch the same bus as him for Brighton station in the morning – at the Sussex Square stop. He of course became much more famous later on as the first 'Doctor Who'.

Jill also got to know Hermione Baddeley, who plays the part of concert artist Ida Arnold in the film. She was the only member of the cast that I said 'Hello' to after Jill had pointed me out to her in front of a crowd of onlookers whilst filming was going on near the Aquarium, and I remember her saying "I know people who'd commit murder to have a head of hair like that!" she was referring to the colour of my hair at that time – which everyone called 'bright red'; I always found remarks about my hair embarrassing – I wouldn't do now if I had any! Jill told me that at times, Hermione – who was one of the old school of actresses and a true 'pro'- sometimes invited some of the extras to have tea with her in her suite at the Grand Hotel; Jill went to a couple of these tea parties, where the conversation flowed brightly, with Hermone – whom everyone called 'Totie' – quickly putting everyone at their ease. "She became a sort of mother figure to us". Jill said. Maire McQueeney mentions this in her 1999 book about the making of the film during the years 1946/47/48 – which is called 'The Brighton Rock Picture Book'. There are a lot of very atmospheric pictures of Brighton in the book – taken at the time filming was going on. Another actor who Jill talked to, was 'Wylie Watson, an excellent 'senior' British character of that era, he plays Spicer in the film – the one that Pinkie pushes to his

108

death over the bannisters! – "He was quiet, very pleasant to talk to and totally unassuming". Said Jill.

When all the location shots had been taken and the extras' work completed, everyone wondered when they would see the finished result, but were told that it probably wouldn't 'come out' until early the next year. As this is a story of a particular year – 1947 – I should really write about the premiere of Brighton Rock in the epilogue, but as I have broken the 'rules' already, by going back into the past at times, I feel it would be more fitting to tell of it now and thus conclude my writings about this film.

The premiere of Brighton Rock took place at the Savoy cinema at mid-night on January 8th 1948. Jill, who sat downstairs with the stars of the film, had given father, Sylvia and me tickets to attend this highly publicised function. Neither Sylvia or father wanted to go at that time of night, and said they'd rather see it at a more reasonable time during the week. It was Uncle Charles who came to my rescue by saying that he would look after the children – my two young cousins Paul and Charles junior – allowing Aunt Daphne a night out – and she and I duly attended the premiere. We missed seeing the stars arriving because we were eager to get to our seats before any last minute rush; we needn't have worried, there were quite a few seats left upstairs, but I believe downstairs was packed. When the film had ended, we went downstairs and said goodnight to Jill, who was going on to a party afterwards – it was then that we saw quite a few of the stars of the film.

As far as the story is concerned, this is fictional – with perhaps a few factual connections. I enjoyed the pier scenes in particular – getting the true atmosphere of Brighton in a film such as this, must have been a very difficult job, and I think the Boulting Brothers did very well, even if some of the scenes were over the top – which of course they were meant to be. As far as Brighton is concerned, this is a subject close to my heart. Brighton is like no other coastal town – or indeed any other town at all. Brighton has a uniquely intriguing atmosphere all of its own; it's not just, as one well known author once told me, "a mix of the Orient, the Casbah and where Mr. and Mrs. Smith slip away to, for a naughty and enjoyable week-end at a town by the seaside, large enough to conceal them from an irate husband or diligent private eye." Brighton is a town that ranges from one end of the social scale to the other, it openly and loudly boasts beautiful, even controversial, buildings, as well as mysterious dwellings in dark and almost forbidden alleys; it is the epitome of cosmopolitan life – and hopefully always will be! More importantly though, there is something about Brighton you can never quite describe – however well you know it. Graham Greene's Brighton of the 1930's has gone, and with it the race course gangs and spivs and drones of that different era. But what's replaced it? – there are plenty of people who have lived in Brighton for a long time, who would like to think they know it intimately, and who, in describing Brighton – 'then and now' – would simply say – " It's a different era – yes, but apart from the different lifestyles at the end of the century, Brighton is still – 'just Brighton!'"

One last thing concerning the film and the premiere. I remember in particular that at that time I had a 'thing' about neckties, and had quite a collection of them – my favourite being the Brighton Tigers tie with its bold black and gold stripes; however, having seen the film, I was very much taken by the tie that Pinkie wore in most of his scenes, so – I hope, more in liking for the tie than the character wearing it – the day after the premiere, with 7/6 burning a hole in my pocket I went in search of a tartan tie – similar to the one worn by Pinkie in the film, and found one for just that price in St. James's Street. A day or two after this I wore it on a trip down town, and was surprised to see that I wasn't the only one wearing such a tie. I noticed, rather disappointingly, as I walked about the town, several young men, all 'attired' similarly – just for a while, tartan ties had taken off!

Returning to the August three day holiday race meeting at Brighton – this was certainly a financial success for the course, if

110

not the bookmakers! During those three days of racing many favourites found their mark, but a lot of these were odds on, and for the 'two bob' punter, such as myself, this wasn't a lot of use! Charlie Smirke, Gordon Richards and his brother Cliff, Eph Smith and Harry Packham were all amongst the winning riders. On the last of these three days the 'angriest' person on the racecourse had to be my Uncle Charles. Father and Charles had decided to give the first day of the meeting a miss; attend the second day in the stands and on the third day go to where Jill and I usually went on the free course near the five furlong gate. In those days – on the Woodingdean side of the rails – there were bookmakers from there to right the way down to the stands. Jill and I would usually go up Wilson's Avenue – a pleasant up hill walk close to the downs – which eventually crosses the race course near the six furlong gate. The bookmakers on the free course would accept bets as low as a shilling to win – even a bob each way – but they were 'wary' of anyone waving a 'white fiver' at them – in those days five pounds wasn't to be sneezed at! There were several bookmakers there – who, if there weren't any policemen around – would take small wagers from teenagers without asking any questions, so we had no trouble in placing our tiny wagers. Jill was too busy to come with me on any of the days of that particular meeting, so I went up with a small group of friends from the square. I finished even on the first day, but lost on the second day, because I didn't think it was worthwhile putting my 'two bobs' on short price favourites – they all won! On the third day, Uncle Charles had been given a tip for a horse called – 'Ann Denise', which was ridden by E. Smith and running in the Brighton Sprint Handicap. He and father had found themselves a position by the rails about a hundred yards down from the five furlong gate; I preferred to stay with my friends at our usual place, right by the starting gate – so we could see the horses close up, listen to the jockey's talking – and even talk to them ourselves!

111

On the first day of the meeting I had 'cheekily' called out to Gordon Richards, who was sitting on a horse not more than five yards away from me – "who's going to win this one Mr. Richards?" It was a silly question to ask of course, but smiling at me he said, "Are you talking to me or him?" – and he pointed to his brother, Cliff, sitting on the horse next to him.

"You" – I answered – surprised that he had even answered me!

"If I knew that son – there wouldn't be much point in running the race would there?!" We laughed with him when he said this.

From that part of the course, it's too far to make out the winning post – yet alone what's won the race; but the bookies with their Tick-Tacks, quickly got the results. On that occasion Gordon's mount – 'Water Boy' had been beaten into second place by his brother's mount – 'Sporting Offer' at the rewarding odds of 4/1 – the beaten Water Boy was favourite for the race at 2 to 1 on – I hadn't backed either of them. On this, the last day of the meeting, Uncle Charles had managed to find a bookmaker who had accepted his five pound bet to win on 'Ann Denise' at odds of seven to four against – this was a quarter of a point better than most of the other bookmakers were offering. Father had placed his bet with a different bookie – only getting six to four against for his ten bob bet. I had put five shillings on at the same odds – this was a large bet for me! 'Ann Denise' duly won this fast run race by a length from Charlie Smirke's mount 'Jambo' – which one of my friends had backed. What happened next I didn't see – but heard about later. Apparently, Uncle Charles, on hearing the result through the 'bush telegraph' – in other words by the tick-tacks – said to father that he was going to collect – father said he'd do likewise. When they got to where the line of bookmakers were, Uncle Charles immediately noticed that at the place where the bookmaker he had backed with had put his board up – there was now just a gap! My uncle immediately got very angry about this – calling out loudly for someone to get the stewards of the course – which of course was ridiculous, as they didn't hold much 'sway' on the free course. My uncle carried on cursing the 'absent' bookmaker – causing quite a rumpus – at the end of the day however he accepted that he'd been 'had' and there was nothing he could do about it – except to loudly proclaim that he'd never use the free course again – he never did! Father lived to tell this tale many times. Just after it had happened he had found it very difficult to stop himself from laughing – but made up for this after Uncle Charles had dropped him off at home. That evening it caused much mirth with some of the locals at the pub – they all thought it was a huge joke!

During those hot summer days, a lot of my time was spent on the beach; I spent so much time in the water that father asked me – "have you started to grow gills yet?" There would usually be a small group of us who used the beach directly below Sussex Square gardens – this was a very long beach which stretched from Black Rock Pool to a breakwater, near which we used to congregate – about three hundred yards to the west of the pool. This particular breakwater served as a good diving platform, if there was a good high tide. I remember playing a rather silly joke from here a few times. The idea was to cause a bit of a panic – with my friends on the beach acting out parts to make the whole thing look convincing. I would dive off the groyne and swim down deeply and away from the beach – under water swimming was my speciality – then I would swim past the end of the groyne, still under water, and re-surface on the next beach. I would then walk up the pebbles and watch what was going on on the beach that I was supposed to be on – where my friends would all be making much of a fuss because I hadn't reappeared from my dive. This would cause some general concern until I would innocently reappear on the beach. I eventually got caught doing this, and got a very loud ticking off – which I thoroughly deserved – from an irate gentleman who had tried to save me!

The next day, it had been arranged that father and I would go fishing on the Palace Pier. In pre-war days father used the landing stage – right at the end of the pier, this was known as the fishermen's deck in those times. He had won three or four fishing competitions from here during the twenties and thirties. His most treasured prize was a set of fish knives and forks – nicely set out in a case with a velvet interior – for catching the rarest fish in a competition. The fish that won him this prize, some people called a 'flying fish'- but I believe that what he caught was a 'gurnard'. On this, our first fishing outing on the pier together in 1947, father decided to fish from the same place, but first, I had had to go to 'Silverlocks', the fishing tackle shop in Duke Street, to get some red rag worms, which Mr. Silverlock put in an empty Players cigarette tin – one that used to hold fifty cigarettes. We arrived at the place father wanted to fish from at mid-day; the platform was quite crowded with people float fishing for mackerel or anything else that might come along – even gar-fish, with their long eel like bodies and pointed 'saw' like noses. These fish could sometimes be seen skimming along the top of the water at some speed, when the mackerel shoals were about and the weather was hot. They made quite good eating and if you filleted one in a darkened kitchen, the backbone would show up green and luminous.

In those days feathers weren't used for catching mackerel, usually just triangular silver coloured metal spinners, with three hooks attached, were the most often used. Fixed spool reels were rare and fibre glass rods were something 'the Americans had invented' and just beginning to show up in England. Our main equipment in those days for sea fishing, were built cane or similar types of rods and big old wooden star backed reels, on which was wound some 'stringy', green coloured salt water line. When the mackerel season was in, the water just in front of the fishing deck on the pier, became a sea of various coloured floats – the trouble was that if a mackerel suddenly took the bait and then darted to one side or the other, it would become entangled with other peoples' lines, thus turning the ozone laden air, blue for a while if it happened frequently – which it did on that day! Father and I fished from the easterly corner of the fishing deck and ignored the mackerel – casting our baits as far out as we could, eventually to sink to the sea bed in the hope of catching flat fish or any other bottom feeding fish. Sport was slow for us that day, with only the odd bite now and again, and by three o'clock we still hadn't caught any fish. The mackerel fishermen were having good sport and catching plenty, but we could catch these from the beaches below Sussex Square – we were after 'bigger and better fry'!

I told father I was going to walk around the pier for a while, and left him to look after both rods. I went into the amusement hall, and as I only had a small amount of pocket money left, I decided to give the penny machines a miss and have a few goes on 'The Kentucky Derby' – a game where you rolled balls up a board to where there were different scoring holes. Above the boards was a race track where you could see your 'horse' moving along according to how much you scored each time your ball went down a hole – first 'horse' to the end of the track won a prize. I spent half a crown on five separate games, and was accurate enough to win twice. On going to collect my prizes, I couldn't make up my mind what I wanted – all the stuff on show was pretty useless to me! Eventually I asked the woman who was handing the prizes out, for two packets of cigarettes – they were a brand I had never heard of before – I think they were foreign. On getting back to father, who was talking to a couple of fishermen he knew slightly, I told him of my success and gave him one of the packets of cigarettes – keeping it secret that I had won two packets. He offered one each to the other men, and remarking that they also hadn't heard of this particular brand before – they lit up. One of the gentlemen, after inhaling a puff went a funny sort of colour and started coughing uncontrollably, the second one after giving me a 'funny' look, as if I'd played some sort of a joke on him, threw his into the sea; father – persevering a puff or two longer than the others, went bright red and also chucked his into the water – saying -"bloody hell!" – Before also going into a fit of coughing. They soon recovered, but father, who also gave me a funny look, said "I know the best place for these" – and chucked what remained of the packet into the sea. Later on, I gave one to my friend Timmy – who, at two years older than me had started smoking at an early age – he admitted that they tasted as if they been manufactured in a farm yard, but said – "they're better than nothing!"

I caught nothing that day, but father had caught a small plaice of about three quarters of a pound. We decided to pack up just after six o'clock. We walked back along the pier, there was no loud music blasting out and the breeze coming off the sea was cooling in the early evening – father remarked to me – "these piers have characters all of their own, and the Palace and West piers are part of Brighton – let's hope they're here forever!"

The day after this, on Saturday August 9th, Jill, as Brighton Summer Queen, with two maids of honour – Mary Bickers and Joy Hadden – had been invited to be guests of honour at Chatham's summer carnival. During the procession through the towns, the car that they were sitting on top of, was stopped by a group of sailors – demanding a ransom! This incident was made much of by the press, including local papers as well as the nationals. There was a picture in the Daily Mirror of the sailors stopping the car and attempting to kiss my sister. Under the heading – 'Beauty Queen Held up in Carnival Drive, Ransom – Three Kisses' the article went on to say:

"Jill Knowles, 18, Brighton Summer Queen, guest of honour at Chatham, (Kent) carnival, was held for ransom in Saturday's procession through the town. Jill, wearing a brief two-piece swim suit was driving through the main street perched on top of a taxi. Three sailors jumped aboard, stopped the taxi and said they would not let the procession go on until they'd kissed – the best looking girl we've seen since we came ashore! For ten minutes the officials tried to reason with the sailors. Then Jill solved the situation and kissed each sailor in turn. By then the naval pickets had arrived, but the sailors didn't care. They jumped off the car shouting "O.K. take us away we've kissed the beauty queen!"

During those summer holidays, Jill attended quite a few functions and her picture often appeared in the papers. At home it had now been accepted that when the phone rang – which was quite often – it was odds on it was for Jill; but we were all enjoying what was going on – it was certainly something different, and after the sadness of the past two years, what with this and Sylvia coming into our lives, some rays of sunshine had penetrated through the gloom, and once again – life was going along quite nicely!

The day after this ,my friend Keith and I spent most of that extremely hot Sunday going for refreshingly cool swims on the least crowded beach we could find – all the beaches were packed! We also spent most of the day making plans for the week to come – the next day was the first day of our long arranged camping holiday at Barcombe Mills. Keith's father, Captain Denyer, had said he would drive us there with all our equipment and collect us the following Sunday – probably coming to see how we were getting on, sometime in between times. We enjoyably got all our fishing tackle ready – making sure everything was in good repair. We spent an hour or so digging in the hard ground of the large garden at the back of number nineteen for worms – much needed bait – we only got a few! We had looked forward to and planned for this special adventure since the previous summer, and at long last the long awaited day was about to dawn.

Chapter Seven

Camping by the Ouse – A general health scare

I saac Walton, admitting that he was quoting some 'wise' Spanish gentleman, once wrote – "Rivers and the inhabitants of the watery element were made for wise men to contemplate and fools to pass by without consideration!"

In Sussex, there are certainly some beautiful rivers to contemplate – each with it's own character . I don't consider myself to be a wise man, but I can certainly sit and contemplate by the quieter stretches of all rivers, including in particular, the Arun in West Sussex, the winding Cuckmere in East Sussex and the 'friendly' River Ouse that flows to the channel at Newhaven.

I find the Sussex Ouse spellbinding – it is a river that holds many memories for me. It begins as a trickle at St. Leonards Forest near Horsham, and stays 'young' until it grows to maturity at Isfield. After this it flows peacefully through Barcombe Mills to a weir, and then the mill pool; after this it is tidal as it continues its journey through Lewes and finally to Newhaven and the sea. It is in the non tidal part of the river, from just above the mill pool to 'Browns' Boathouse that I had discovered a place which, to me, was a mixture of tranquillity, beauty, sport and some of nature at it's best, and it was beside a stretch of the river here that we would set up camp.

I awoke very early on Monday 11th August 1947 – had a quick breakfast and then spent the next two hours re-checking that I had got everything that was needed for the camping holiday. A little later, after saying goodbye to Sylvia and father, I carried all my equipment, including a box of food that Sylvia had prepared for me, over to number nineteen Sussex Square, where I found Keith and his father busily getting all Keith's equipment, including the tent, into the car. At just before eleven o'clock – with Keith's mother joining us for "a nice trip into the country," – we left off from the square and eventually took the road for Lewes and our eventual destination, Barcombe Mills. I had only come this way once before by car, and that was before the war. Keith and I had come here together on several occasions by train in 1946, and earlier in 1947, and each time we'd been fascinated by everything we had seen – including the isolated old station. This little country stop, which in those days was still used by steam trains, ran between Tunbridge Wells and Brighton, stopping at Uckfield and Isfield, amongst other stations on the down journey, before arriving at Barcombe Mills.

George Farenden the signalman, who was more of a general factotum – in that, he sold and collected the tickets, operated the crossing gates by hand, went around lighting the gas lights at dusk and kept the place clean and tidy. When Keith and I had first waited at the station after a day on the river, we had been intrigued to see him carrying a long wooden pole with a hook on the end, from light to light to switch the gas on, by pulling down on the end of a chain on one side of the lamp, which then lighted up. He, of course, reversed this procedure to turn it off. A couple of minutes or so before the up train was due, a bell would ring, then ring again, and Mr. Farenden would then walk over to the crossing gates and open them. After the train had gone he would open the gates again, allowing any cars that were waiting to continue on their journey – there weren't many of those on that quiet country road in those days. Keith and I would then have another ten minutes or so before the down train arrived, and as the summers night drew in, we watched the bats as they flittered about – almost too close to us – and soon, as an owl called out from somewhere near the river, we would hear the haunting whistle of the train in the distance, which told us our means of getting home would soon arrive. Living in the town, we found it a wrench to leave this 'paradise' and, in thinking in such a way, the first plans for a camping holiday had started to take shape in our imaginative minds.

Keith's father stopped the car near the bank of a stretch of the river about a quarter of a mile from the boathouse. Just across the river from there, there is a slim 'peninsula' of land that we called 'pike point', where the river divides into two stretches; we had decided to camp here – 'far from the madding crowd' – or to be more precise, the dozen or so people who had put up tents in the recognised camping field, close to the boathouse. The idea was, instead of carrying all our gear across the fields from the boathouse, we would hire one of the flat bottom canoes and paddle up river to where the car was, and then ferry all the equipment across the water. This minor operation was duly carried out, without a hitch, and an hour after delivering us to what would be our home for the next few days, Keith's parents left two highly excited youths to erect the tent, store the food we had brought with us safely, put the fishing tackle together – and then start exploring the river in the canoe, which Mr. Denyer had paid at the boathouse for us to keep for another two hours.

The Browns had bought this land and the boathouse where they all lived, back in the nineteen thirties; they had started hiring out the canoes three years after they had arrived – it wasn't until later years that they started to increase the farm's livestock. They had also made the ground floor room that overlooks the river, into a tearoom, open to the public. People who didn't have cars in those days, who visited this quiet stretch of the river – and that was the majority of them – would have to walk from the station along a small winding road which eventually joined a rough track that led to the boathouse. On either side of the track, as one walked up here, there were grazing fields and hedgerows, with various types of trees growing close to the riverbank. The only buildings in sight were the barns of a farmyard one passed through near the beginning of this walk; these are part of Curds Farm, owned by the Cornwell family who came here to farm in 1892. In the quieter times of the year, especially of course in the winter, you could fish all day from the river bank and not see another soul – only the sound of the occasional steam train going past, a mile or so away, reminded one of civilisation – all other sounds, nature provided.

We spent the rest of the time we had the hire of the canoe for exploring the stretches of the river that we were able to get to, including some of the little 'tributaries' where we liked to imagine that other canoes seldom ventured. We soon got to know the 'secret' places on the river, including widening pools that appeared every now and again on our journey – these, we made mental notes to remember to fish at some other time. We were constantly aware of the beauty of the river and always alert to the wildlife around us.

In his book 'The England I Love Best,' James Turle wrote, " – Of all the Sussex rivers, I think the Ouse is the one that leads first into the heart of Sussex. For the Ouse is a kind river; a river that will take you to her heart and teach you to love her, and she will leave with you a little of that spirit of the Ouse, which once given – can never be wholly lost."

The weather remained hot and sunny throughout all the days of that camping holiday; we fished for a lot of the time, sometimes from different places along the river bank, sometimes from a canoe, and sometimes whilst precariously balanced from some branch of a tree that overlooked a tempting pool, which was impossible to get at any other way.

Father and Sylvia came out on one of the days we were there – as did Keith's mother and father and his younger brother David. I remember that father spent quite a lot of the time sketching near to where we were camping – probably a scene that had taken his eye that day, and which eventually, back at home, he would make into a water colour painting. Keith's mother was also an artist – quite exceptional in fact. She painted lifelike pictures of flowers and other subjects – all of these in oil. She got some recognition for her paintings, which I very much admired – as did father and Sylvia and everyone else who saw them.

Many keen anglers went to Barcombe Mills to fish for sea trout; these pink fleshed members of the salmon family would come up the river from the sea at Newhaven, eventually reaching the non-tidal stretches where they would spawn. The mill pool was the place mainly used by the fishermen for these fish – this is where the tidal and non-tidal parts of the river are divided. Father only fished the non-tidal stretches though, and throughout the years I can only remember him catching three of these elusive fish. A man whose name became synonymous with catching sea trout, was Dan Wilson – a well known name for fishing the Ouse, and in the days before the war an acquaintance of father's. Another person who also spent a lot of time trying to catch these wily fish whilst walking the banks of the river, was Magnus Volk, the man who invented and built the railway on Brighton seafront; he also had a small caravan near the boathouse where he would spend a peaceful night or two, from time to time.

Although we tried hard, Keith and I didn't catch a sea trout during that camping holiday, but at night, while we were sitting contentedly by a small camp fire, with no other sounds coming from the darkness other than our own voices and perhaps the occasional call of an owl or a train whistling in the distance – suddenly the silence of the river would be broken by the sound of a heavy splash, letting us know that a sea trout was probably making a journey up or down river – taking a snack now and again, as it went on it's way.

Sometimes, shortly after we'd had tea and before we'd fished the 'evening rise' we would walk down to the pub next door to the station. We were too young, of course, to buy any alcoholic beverage, but the landlord who knew father as a customer, would serve us with ginger beer or something similar despite our age, as long as there were no other customers about at the time – which at that time in the evening was likely to be the case! We usually sat on a bench just outside the pub, but he allowed us to sit in the tiny snug bar if we wanted. In those days, in particular in that pub, there were no juke boxes or fruit machines. Whilst we sat there, the only ornamentation we could see was a stuffed pike in one glass case and a perch in another one; both of these skilfully 'mounted' with a background of what looked like their natural surroundings. Sometimes when we were there, Mr. Stephenson, the landlord, would tell us tales of the river, and even tell us stories of when he used to be a 'hangman' in the army in Egypt!

On a couple of occasions during those camping days, when we got fed up with our own cooking, we'd go to the boathouse tearoom, where Mrs. Brown would serve us with boiled, new laid eggs from her own hens – which could be seen running around more or less wherever they pleased. Another animal attraction here were the monkeys – three of them kept as pets and obviously quite an attraction to everyone visiting the boathouse; They could be seen sitting or clambering about in the trees nearby. There was an African Grass Monkey, a Rhesus Monkey and a Capuchin – which is a very intelligent breed of monkey – this one in particular fascinated Keith and me, with its 'near to human' antics and expressions.

All too quickly the days of our first camping adventure came to a close, and on another hot summer's day Keith's parents, once again bringing David with them, arrived to spend the afternoon by the river and in the early evening, drive us back to Brighton.

During the time we had been away – on Friday August 15th it had been reported in all the papers that after 163 years – British rule in India was now at an end. To mark this momentous occasion, one paper said – 'a conch shell was blown in the Constituent Assembly in New Delhi amid cheers from the members as the hands ticked away the seconds to the independence for which the Indians have striven for so long.' The article continues – 'Lord Mountbatten, who relinquished the panoply of empire as Britain's last envoy, and immediately became governor-general of the new dominion of India, has been rewarded by a grateful government in London, with an Earldom for his part in expertly managing Britain's retreat. One of his last acts as viceroy was to deliver a moving message of congratulations from King George Vl to the people of Pakistan saying – "I send you my greetings and warmest wishes on this great occasion when the new dominion of Pakistan is about to take it's place in the British Commonwealth of nations. In thus achieving your independence by agreement you have set an example to the freedom loving peoples throughout the world."

The celebrations were marred by violence – even independence cannot end racial hatred!'

Father told me that a few extra glasses were raised at the pub on that evening – friends or acquaintances who had seen service in India. Some raised their glasses to say goodbye to what had been a way of life in India; but the majority toasting the successful conclusion to this long and bitter feud. "One thing"- father said - " that we had all agreed on, was that the next few months were going to be the 'tricky' ones, and 'policing' this vast area was going to be no picnic, and It was going to be interesting to see how powerful the influence of Mahatma Gandhi was going to be!

During the next few days I spent most of my time swimming and fishing from the beaches immediately below Sussex Square and Chichester Terrace. Sometimes I tried spinning for mackerel from the breakwaters, and on one particular, day father and I even tried catching them from the landing stage of the Palace Pier. There were so many people fishing for mackerel from here that we almost gave up before we started. Fishermen's lines kept crossing other peoples lines as they hooked fish – when this happened it usually provoked a good deal of cursing from the other fishermen – usually in none too delicate language! After father had seen the only two mackerel that he'd caught, drop off back into the sea because of crossed lines, he decided to call it a day. I found it difficult to control my laughter as father stumped off the pier exclaiming that the whole thing was "bloody madness" and added, " I can think of more enjoyable ways of spending my time!" The mackerel shoals were now coming in in plenty all along the Sussex coast; the hot weather had brought huge accumulations of white bait close into the shore in many places, and of course the mackerel followed these in. Just for a while they became too easy to catch, so that father and I felt rather ashamed that we'd even thought of trying on the pier. There was a report that on one of the hottest days – at Hastings – one enterprising man waded into the water, chest deep, carrying an empty bucket and returned to the beach with the bucket full of still lively fish!

I went prawning on several occasions in the rock pools on the beaches between Black Rock and Ovingdean – on one occasion, even as far as Rottingdean. I had some good catches which were quickly cooked and soon eaten, together with fresh baked bread and butter – delicious!

George Robinson, who now lives near Hastings, also spent the whole of the summer of 1947 close to the beaches. In a letter to me, after the Hastings and Bexhill Observer had printed an article about my writing this book, asking for anyone with special memories of 1947 in Sussex, to contact me, he writes:

"I spent the war years in the army – the Desert Rats; eventually, in 1944 whilst back in Blighty after I'd been wounded, I got married; three weeks later I got a letter saying my wife had been killed by a 'doodlebug' – her mother had been killed as well. A bit later I heard that my brother had been killed, whilst serving in the Royal Navy. By the time I was demobbed, with the rank of sergeant, in 1946 I had no close relatives left – my father had died before the war, so I was on my own. For the rest of that year and the early months of 1947 I tried my hand at more than a dozen different jobs – some lasting a few days, some a few weeks. One only lasted two hours, when I told some 'over officious' young foreman exactly where he could put his job! I was going through a difficult time, and being something of a loner and fiercely trying to remain independent, I just drifted from job to job, hoping to find something I liked, which would last – but I wasn't having much luck and even thought of signing up with the army again, but this would have meant losing my independence once more.

Eventually, in April 1947, I hitched a lift to Eastbourne where I worked in a hotel kitchen for a week. I packed that in after drawing a week's money – which wasn't very much. I remember I walked out of the town; I had a large holdall, in which were all my worldly possessions. I had intended to thumb a lift to Hastings and try my luck there, but lifts weren't forthcoming and I walked all the way into Pevensey Bay, where I stopped for what I thought would be an hour or two at most – but turned out to be for the rest of the summer. I had gone into the public bar of one of the local pubs and got talking to another ex-serviceman whilst drinking my pint and eating a couple of rounds of sandwiches. He told me how he made something of a living by going out with the local fishermen when they needed an extra hand, and at other times by doing odd jobs for local people – even working behind various bars for a few hours each week. By doing such things he found he could make ends meet and at the same time, more or less keep his independence. He told me that he'd spent the whole of the war being bossed about, and he'd had enough of it! I envied the man his way of life, and seeing that I hadn't got anything else lined up, I there and then decided I would try and do much the same sort of thing!

For the first two nights I slept rough in an empty boat on the beach; this was just near to Normans Bay – about a mile along the coast from Pevensey Bay. In the daytime I watched an old boy as he laid 'long lines' on the sand at low tide, and was fascinated to see the fish that he'd caught on his baited hooks when he went to collect any catch that might be there, after the tide had come in and gone out again. During that week I went

126

into Eastbourne and managed to buy a cheap second hand tent and a sleeping bag. I also bought a lot of loose hooks and fishing line, including some stronger stuff for the actual long lines. I decided I would camp somewhere near to The Crumbles – a long pebbly area between Pevensey Bay and Langney Point, just outside Eastbourne. In those days this was a rather desolate area, with the odd pillbox here and there, left over from wartime. I decided to try my luck at this for a week or two and see how I got on. I had also bought myself a second hand garden fork for digging the 'blow lug' whose casts you could see in profusion on the beaches where I planned to lay my lines. The beaches along this stretch were lonelier than the ones at Pevensey Bay – but I wasn't the only one trying to eke out a living here, in this way. All you did was lay out your lines with about twenty hooks on each line – there was what we call a snood between the hook and the main line. I would lay these on sand banks – quite well out, then tie each end of the line to a block of wood or sturdy piece of drift wood, which could be found in abundance on the beaches, then bury them in the sand so the line was tight, bait the hooks, cover them with sand so the gulls couldn't get at them and then wait for the tide to come in. At the next low tide, whilst waiting to see what I'd caught, I would dig more blow lug, which I used to re-bait the hooks – and so on. Any fish that I caught, such as plaice or soles, I would sell to a chef I had got to know in an Eastbourne hotel. I also bought myself a large shrimping net – about seven ft. across – but the shrimps were mainly small at that time of year, so I didn't have much success there.

I didn't earn enough money from all this to keep myself going – it was a precarious way to make a living, and sometimes the catches were negligible, so I took on doing odd jobs for people who lived near to the beaches. I even took on painting someone's house; I never scrounged for anything!

I slept in that tent for nearly two months – then moved into a rented room nearby, not far from the beach. While I lived there I could come and go as I pleased – so I still kept my independence, which for some reason seemed so important to me at that time.

During those hot summer months, I used to go on long walks and got to know the coastline and beaches at Birling Gap and Beachy Head in a westerly direction, and Normans' Bay to Cooden Beach in the east. Feeling very low at one time, I even went into the tiny church at Normans' Bay and prayed – it seemed to do some good!

I am now near to eighty years of age, and my wife, children and grandchildren and me, still visit these beautiful stretches of coastline, even if they have changed a bit, what with a marina where the crumbles were and other things – but there's still the beauty there.

Towards the end of that unforgettable summer, I met my wife Iris for the first time – that was in Eastbourne, on the pier. We married a year later and eventually I got a steady job on a farm, with a cottage to go with it. I spent the rest of my working life on three different Sussex farms – eventually buying the house I still live in with my wife. All of this became possible for me from what happened in the most memorable year of my life – 1947. When my wife saw in the local paper that someone was writing a book about 1947 – you could have knocked me down with a feather – and I felt I just had to write this letter, I hope it's of use to you!"

Just about every day during that memorable August was a sunny one, and the temperatures fluctuated from pleasantly warm to downright hot! It was a 'dream' summer, but like a lot of other things in life when the 'going is good' – there was also a downside, and at that time the big worry was the increasing numbers in the infantile paralysis outbreak. Uncle Jimmy, who was still working as a lifeguard for the summer season at Black Rock Bathing Pool, told us that during the last two or three weeks it was noticeable that people were keeping away, and the numbers attending the pool had dropped dramatically. On one of the early days of the holidays I went with a couple of friends to see Uncle Jimmy at work, the sea was a bit rough that day in any case, and we had a quick dip in an almost empty pool. On another day I arranged to meet a friend at the open air pool, on the undercliff walk at Rottingdean. I remember my mother taking me to this pool in 1945, and found it a very pleasant place for a swim, but on this occasion my friend and I and four or five other people, were the only ones who were using it during the two hours we were there. The reports in the papers confirmed that the numbers of people catching this crippling and sometimes fatal disease, was on the increase throughout the country, and The Ministry of Health had issued a warning saying it was best to avoid crowded places such as, bathing pools, cinemas and any other places which were likely to attract large numbers of holiday makers; consequently a lot of these places were badly hit by diminishing attendances. In the bathing pools it was felt that the disease would 'linger' in the water, but the beaches remained crowded because it was widely felt that the germs wouldn't spread in tidal waters. It was a time for vigilance, but with the good weather still carrying on, many people were still tempted to make hay whilst the sun shone – despite the 'lurking' dangers.

Later in August, Brighton held its summer festival, and Jill as Summer Queen had to attend many of the events taking place, in an official capacity. Anchored just off Brighton during the festival was one of the Royal Navy's most up to date destroyers – H.M.S. St. James. Jill went aboard this ship – ferried there and back by the Brighton pleasure boat, 'The Montgomery'. On board, the sailors had a pet mascot – a very lively bull terrier called Jimmy; unfortunately when Jill bent down to stroke the dog and make a fuss of it, the dog decided to jump up and make a fuss of her, and in so doing, they bumped noses – making Jill's nose bleed. The press had a field day with this, saying that the dog had bitten her, even though she had let it be known very clearly to the crew and everyone else who was there at the time, that the dog hadn't bitten her and it was just an accident. The press chose to ignore this and the whole thing was misreported – which made Jill very angry; but the dog remained as mascot on board the ship for quite a long time after this – at least the sailors knew the truth!

On the 26th August, a brilliant summer's day with a nice sea breeze cooling things down to make it "ideal weather for walking on the downs" – as father put it, wishing he still had the use of both of his legs – I decided to take his advice and have one of my rambles over the downs to Ovingdean and Rottingdean. I took a picnic lunch with me and left off from home at just after 11am. Whilst walking just near the back of Rottingdean I noticed there were a lot of policemen all over the place – they seemed to be looking for something or someone. I stopped to see what was going on at the same time as observing a group of farm workers building a straw stack – it was harvesting time; there were several policemen standing here watching the workers as well. A sergeant asked me if I'd seen any suspicious looking men about and advised me not to go back home the way I had intended – over the downs. He said that they were looking for two men who were armed and highly dangerous. The odd thing was that during the war years, when I was out looking for owls nests with my friend Timmy, we had been stopped by police not far from here; that time they were also looking for two suspicious characters – probably deserters. One doesn't expect to find the police patrolling the downs, but this time there was a greater air of urgency about the whole thing, and I decided to walk back along the overcliff walk – hopefully keeping out of the way of any modern day outlaws. In the Evening Argus that day the headlines were:

"Bandits Hold up Post Office at Brighton" and went on to say – "One of the biggest manhunts in the history of Sussex was still going on this evening as scores of police searched the Sussex downs for two armed bandits. The men, masked with scarves and carrying automatic pistols, forced their way into the bedroom of 'The Stores', Lustrells-Vale, Saltdean, shortly after 6am today.' The article went on to say – 'three chief constables in their shirt sleeves were out with the squads of detectives and uniformed police. Many police were armed. Patrols of police who were drawn from Brighton and East Sussex, flushed the downland area on foot, while patrol cars covered the main Eastbourne – Brighton and main Newhaven – Lewes roads. All buses and vehicles on the coast road were stopped and searched.' Before they broke into the stores, the bandits cut the telephone wires. After the hold-up they escaped over the downs with their loot – just £50; but of course it was because they were armed that it caused such a widespread alert.

The outcome of all this was that the manhunt went on for a couple of days or so, with the fugitives eventually being captured. As far as the press were concerned, the whole of this episode paled into insignificance when another manhunt hit the headlines the next day, and this one certainly set my father and a lot of other people thinking. The headline said – 'Sussex forest combed for three men.' The report went on to say – 'Three German POW's at large since last Thursday, when they escaped from a working party at a Billingshurst camp, were being hunted today in the Houghton Forest area near Arundel, where they have already been seen. A man believed to be a deaf and dumb Pole, was mistaken for one of the fugitives today and chased and tied up by a farmer and his men. When the police arrived the mistake was realised. The German are believed to be hiding in the caves in Houghton Forest, which were built in the event of invasion. Police and armed soldiers are intensively combing the area'.

There were still plenty of German prisoners of war working on the land and other 'labouring type' jobs in various parts of the country in 1947. The main question that people were asking at that time – including my father, was – "is this still really necessary?" The general feelings were, 'Surely as they were just soldiers doing their duty during the war, they would be better off back in their own country now – helping to rebuild from the ashes of the devastating bombing or doing anything else where labour was needed in their defeated country!' I remember father saying at that time – "the politics in these matters are beyond my understanding!"

These Germans were soon back at the POW camp, with the headlines having a field day in some different direction.

Escaping prisoners, were mostly an exception to the rule, and although there were many fanatical Nazis among the POW's in the camps across the country who did escape, or try to escape from time to time, there were many more who hated what Nazism stood for and were quite pleased to be where they were – and away from the turmoil of war! There were reports from all over the country of how well many of these POW's worked on the farms and other places. There were also many friendships struck up, lasting 'till well after repatriation had come for them – sometimes for life.

Dorothy and Philip Roebotham farmed seventy acres of land at Lattinden's Farm, near Bexhill – this was on the Ashburnham Estate, owned by Lady Katherine Ashburnham. Because of the wartime need for every bit of available land being used to grow things for the war effort, they rented a further seventy five acres from the estate, and farmed this as well. The farm was a mix of dairy and arable, with plenty of barley and wheat being grown. To get the extra labour they needed for this, they simply applied to the nearest offices of the wartime Ministry of Agriculture for prisoners of war to come and work on the farm – and got them. Eventually, after they'd had POW's working with them for some time, one particular prisoner arrived to work there, who literally, as Philip and Dorothy told me, "became part of the family!" He was one of the prisoners from Normanhurst Camp near Battle – his name is Bernard Timmer – Timmy, to them. At first he had to go to and fro from the camp each day, under escort, as did the other prisoners. Eventually however, Philip and Dorothy got permission for him to live in with them – he just had to report back to camp once a month. He worked there until he was repatriated, and that included right through 1947.

According to Philip and Dorothy, they never had any trouble with any of the prisoners – they were all very good workers. After Timmy got married in Germany in 1953, he and his young bride came to England and spent their honeymoon on the farm. Timmy went on to become an accomplished engineer; he still visits Philip and Dorothy at their quiet and lovely home at Bexhill, it has become a special friendship and they still think of him as one of the family.

I still found plenty to do during my summer holiday – including going swimming at least once every day. The mackerel shoals were swimming close to the shores, and the anglers on the breakwaters were becoming quite used to taking home bags full of fresh fish – "wouldn't this have come in handy during the war years when fish was so scarce and expensive?" Father said.

In the Brighton and Hove Gazette on 30th August there were three pictures of my sister doing her duty as Beauty Queen. In one she was pictured by the side of Howard Pyper, the owner of a Brighton engineering firm – he was dressed as Adolf Hitler – they were collecting money for SSAFA, (soldiers', sailors' and airmen's families association). In the second one she was presenting a cup to the winners of the Brighton Brass Band Festival, to Mrs. B.Evans of the Toddington Town Band – Jill had travelled to Toddington in Bedfordshire to present this cup. The third photograph showed Jill dressed for a film part which was supposed to be in pre-historic times – the Gazette said – "clad in a leopardskin, Brighton Summer Queen, Jill Knowles, became a film actress for a day on Tuesday – as a cave woman. She was playing a role in the Keystone Film Production Units 'Fighting Spirit' – shooting of which was taking place in various parts of Sussex this week. The film deals with the history of boxing, and in the sequence in which Miss.Knowles appeared – which was made at Hastings – shots were taken of primitive men fighting for a mate."

On September 3rd the news from India was that Ghandi – still trying to persuade his followers that passive resistance instead of

133

violence was the best way – disappointed that this was not being kept to, was still on hunger strike, and was now very weak.

On September 8th news came through that the Jewish refugees on the ship 'Exodus' had disembarked at Hamburg – "the mind boggles!" Father said at breakfast that morning.

A tune that everyone seemed to be whistling and singing at that time was " Oh! What a Beautiful Morning" which came from the musical 'Oklahoma!' Both this famous musical and 'Annie Get Your Gun' had opened in London during 1947. I had been invited to go and see 'Oklahoma' at the Theatre Royal, Drury Lane by the mother of a friend of mine who lived at Queens Park, Peter Collier – his mother had been a well known opera singer. Despite this meaning that I would have to mingle with a large crowd during the height of the infantile paralysis epidemic, I had gladly accepted the invitation – as father said – "Life must go on!" We thoroughly enjoyed this great musical – it was my first 'big show' night in London. Three years later I would go and see 'Annie Get Your Gun,' on a special night out celebrating Jill's 21st birthday.

The day after seeing 'Oklahoma' I 'mingled' with another large crowd – this time at a special cricket match at Hastings, for which father had got tickets, but once again, because of trouble with his leg, felt that it would be unwise to go to. Consequently I was given the two tickets, and with my friend Michael, we caught the train from Brighton to Hastings – where a special festival of cricket week was taking place. During that day we watched Dennis Compton make 87 in his second innings for the 'South of England' team against Sir Pelham Warner's X1 – he had made 86 not out in the first innings, but even these two superb pieces of batting entertainment weren't enough, and 'Plum' Warner's team were the winners by just 26 runs. In that match, Compton passed Tom Hayward's record aggregate of 3,518 runs in a season – made in 1906. Bowling in the match that day against the south, was a young man called Laker – he had taken six of the South's second innings wickets for 109 runs, and I heard one gentleman sitting near to me comment – "We'll be hearing more of him!"

This was the only time that I attended a match at that ground in the centre of Hastings – now unfortunately a shopping centre and something of the past.

On arriving home, I was told that Uncle Charles and Aunt Daphne were coming to see us the following weekend. They were going to invite me for a trip out into the country with my two young cousins – Charles junior and Paul. Sylvia told me that they were going to a place called Drusillas, near Alfriston – a small zoo with a well known tearoom, which was a meeting place for people with cars in the days when there weren't too many of these on the roads, in the 1920's and 30's. I could just about remember mother and father driving Jill and me there in the 1930's. I looked forward to this outing, but I didn't want the days between now and then to pass too quickly – I was well aware that there were now only nine days left before it was 'return to school time'. The summer holidays were nearly at an end, but I intended to make full use of all the days remaining.

Chapter Eight

A letter from West Sussex – Some tipsy gentlemen.
The kestrel that went to war

In 1947, many people who had served in the armed forces during the war, were beginning to settle back into civilian life – quite a lot of them not 'demobbed' until 1946. A house of one's own to live in, was a very difficult thing to find for couples where one or both partners were just out of uniform, and although ex-service people had had the promise of priority, the waiting lists were long and frustrating for nearly all concerned. Many couples found accommodation with relatives, but these were usually in cramped quarters and they ached for a place of their own, especially, of course, if there were any young children, or if, as was more often the case, the first born was on the way.

My Uncle Jimmy – an ex Desert Rat – had none of these worries, but was still unsettled. He had decided though that when he had finished his summer stint at Black Rock bathing pool, he would give London a try and look for work which might help him in the writing he most wanted to do. For another ex Desert Rat – born in, and still living in Sussex – things were very different.

Jack and Audrey O'Neill had married in 1942; Jack – demobbed in 1946 – had served for six years in the 4/5th Royal Sussex Regiment, and had fought in North Africa, including at El Alamein, and after that in Iraq. Audrey had served for five years in the WAAFS – they had both served their country well. There were no houses available to them to rent, so they put their names down on five different waiting lists. Ex service personnel were supposed to get preference, but the lists were long and consequently they lived with Jacks' parents in a thatched cottage at Wepham, which is close to the village of Burpham near Arundel. This is a very beautiful part of the county with picture postcard views – they loved the area very much and wanted to stay there, and even though a child was on the way they decided to opt for independence – despite there being nothing available that they might call their own for a while; that is until they discovered that nearby there was an old hut that had been used by the army during the war – now deserted and empty. They decided to squat in this makeshift accommodation, but also tell the council that this was what they were going to do. The council decided that this was okay, and did one or two small jobs for them to make the hut more habitable – also, to make the whole thing official – charge them ten shillings a week rent. There was electric light already laid on, but there were no points for electric fires. The whole thing was "a very enjoyable adventure – something never to be forgotten." Audrey told me. She described those times in 1947 in a letter to me, and I feel the descriptions should be left to her. She writes:

"1947, was an important year for us. There were no houses for 'returning heroes,' so we lived with my husband's parents in a very old thatched cottage at Wepham, near Arundel. In January 1947 we moved into an old army hut (deserted after the war) on the edge of Burpham. Our daughter was born in Arundel Cottage Hospital on Valentines Day. The hut was freezing cold, with only a small kitchen range for heating and cooking; we were lucky because we did have a cold water tap! We had an old flat iron to heat on the stove, and our bath was a tin tub in front of the range. The oven had no heat control, so sometimes the cakes were burnt. Every week I black leaded the stove – our 'lavvi' was an 'Elsan' in the shed. Most of our furniture, cutlery, china etc. was either second hand or utility. Many things were in short supply, we still had ration books. Our washing was done by hand, with the aid of a bar of soap and a scrubbing board!

I remember that bitter winter and the long hot summer very well. The snow drifted to the tops of the hedgerows and we woke in the morning to find snow in the kitchen. In the summer, Jack had to hose down our tin roof to keep cool. We had spiders spinning down from the rafters and earwigs dropping onto the lino. We had a small plot of land behind the hut where we grew flowers and vegetables. Jack was a lorry driver, working for Mr. Silverlock in Arundel. His wage was £4 per week – quite good money in 1947."

Audrey goes on to explain about food deliveries from the International Stores or the Co-op, these were once a week, "– so you placed your order for next week's food a week ahead of time. There was a village shop that sold everything from boot laces to birthday cards, and we bought some of our food here – it was also a post office and a meeting place! There was a blacksmith and carpenters, and if you wanted to order anything that wasn't available in the village, Paynes of Arundel delivered orders every two weeks. Sometimes we'd go to the cinema in Arundel – but the buses only ran on three evenings of the week.

During the summer of 1947 there was no regular bus service so we bought a pre-war Morris Eight car from Jack's boss. It was lovely having the hood down and driving to Climping. There were no car parks – even in 1947 – just parking on the roadside near the sea; no holiday crowds and empty beaches!"

Audrey concludes her letter by saying, – "1947, was, for us a very happy and peaceful year. I love the country life and village people, the bleating of sheep and lambs on the downs, and the song of the nightingale. I even loved our little hut – our first home."

When Audrey talks of trips to Climping, this reminds me of Jill and me being driven there on quite a few occasions in the thirties; also in an open topped car – sometimes driven by mother after father had had his leg amputated and was unable to drive. I remember it was where the countryside came down to the sand and there were hardly any people there. Mother used to describe it as "just beautiful" – it was one of her favourite places.

Some more people who were trying to settle into normal life again after the war, were a small group that included my Uncle Charles. He, with Nicky Marcy, who lived at 23 Sussex Square and who was a good friend of my father's, were set on creating and starting their own business, if only they could 'hit' on the right idea – something that no one else had thought of! Uncle Charles, having lost a leg at Arnhem, and with a fiery temperament, wasn't exactly easy to employ – he was another one who very much liked his independence. He, Nicky and a friend of theirs, Jimmy Knowland, whose family Knowland Brothers ran several well known Brighton pubs, had already failed in a couple of ventures. At that time Jimmy Knowland still retained an interest in the family business, but was also something of an adventurer. After the first failures, they eventually struck on the idea of cleaning the telephones of offices, shops etc. – they called the business Saniphone. For a while, this business was fairly successful – it certainly kept them working – even Jill, when she wasn't modelling, helped out. After a while, it became evident though that this new idea wasn't going to earn them a fortune – business had started to decline, and whilst it was still limping along they started looking for anything else which might do considerably better. In the long run, it turned out that they were never very successful at anything they put their hands to, together! During the time that they were doing all this, there was one incident that did lead to their meeting some people who eventually had considerably better fortune in creating and starting a business in the early years after the war.

Uncle Charles arrived in the square one day and said that he, Nicky Marcy and Jimmy Knowland were going in his and Jimmy's cars to collect some special new types of cider and wine that was being made at Horam – not too far from Eastbourne. Jimmy Knowland had heard of this place from a friend of his who had told him that one of the partners in this new firm – which was called Merrydown – had been a prisoner of war and had thought up the idea for this business while held captive. Whether this was true or not, he couldn't say, but in any case it would be an interesting run out there, and if the stuff that they were making was any good, he might be able to introduce some to the Knowland Bros. pubs, and one or two other pubs where he knew the landlords well. "You never know" he said, "there could even be a profit in it!"

They offered to take father with them, but he declined saying, "I'll have a taste of whatever it is you bring back though!"

That evening, with the three adventurers safely back home, having successfully purchased what they wanted, there was an impromptu get together at Nicky Marcy's flat – father and Sylvia were invited, but only father went. With other invitations that had hastily gone out, there was a party of nine people. By the end of a three hour get together – they were nine very 'tight' people. They were still just about in control of themselves to behave as gentlemen – but none the less, 'tight.'

The next day, at home, father said to us, "this is a very good drink, but something to treat with respect and not drink like ordinary bottled cider." Father went on to tell of the prisoner of war part of the 'Merrydown' business, and told us an interesting – if not complete story of how this new firm had got going. I remember only a tiny bit of what he told us that day in 1947, but because this book is about that year, I thought I would pursue the matter a bit further and find out what I could by contacting 'Merrydown' at Horam. This is their story – very much in brief:

There were two originators of the Merrydown firm, which makes vintage cider and wines – they were Ian Howie and Jack Ward. In 1946 they were joined by John Kellond-Knight, and these three established the company. Their paths had diverged in pre-war days. Jack Ward was four years older than both Ian Howie and John Kellond-Knight, but fate brought them together at an early age. The Kellond-Knights were friends of Dr. and Mrs. Robert Howie, Dr.Howie being in general practice in Eastbourne; Mrs. Ward was friendly with Mrs. Howie. In the late 1930's – because of a shared interest in wine and cider making, they had talked of the possibilities of going into business together. The war was to interrupt any further planning.

Jack Ward had tried to join the Royal Navy, but had been turned down because of a heart murmur. He had been able to pursue his wine-making activities during the war, but because of the shortage of ingredients – particularly sugar – this was on a very limited scale. Ian Howie had served with the Westminster Dragoons before volunteering to join an amateur ski battalion in the 5th Scots Guards. After this he was commissioned into the 3rd County of London Yeomanry – but got separated from that regiment and sent out to North Africa with the 2nd Armoured Division. He was eventually taken prisoner just near Tobruk and handed over to the Italians – when the Italian armistice came, they were taken over by the Germans on the same night. Ian and some other officers, when they were being moved to Germany, made an almost successful escape at Innsbruck station.

He says – "we were in cattle trucks, – I cut a hole in the top of ours, put my legs out, and when nothing happened two of us got out, followed by another one. We simply began walking. When we were challenged on the bridges, where there were sentries, we said we were workers – and kept going like that for days. We were within four kilometers of the Swiss frontier when we were caught – by the Austrian Home guard, of all people!" Later on, whilst at Oflag VIIIF in Germany, Ian carried on making a sort of wine from raisins and sugar – this went down very well with the prisoners, but they had an almost impossible task hiding what he was doing from his captors. He was eventually liberated by the Americans in 1945. It is this part of the story which had eventually led to it being thought that Merrydown cider had been 'invented' in a prisoner of war camp.

John Kellond-Knight had joined the Royal Navy Volunteer Reserve, and had found himself posted to Admiralty work; he went to Africa for a while after the war but eventually returned to Sussex in 1946. It was in that year that they formed the company – each of them putting up £100. Later on, when they were 'stumped' for thinking up a name for the firm, it was Ian who suddenly proclaimed that the ideal name would be the same as that on the gatepost of Jacks home at Rotherfield – Merrydown!

In 1947 they moved their makeshift premises of a nissen hut to Horam Manor, which after a fire in 1941 needed a lot doing to it. However, the space they needed was there and the old oast house could be converted into flats for the families.

It would take too long here to explain how they got on with the actual making of the cider. For marketing, they spent a considerable amount of time going from pub to pub in London, Brighton and other places, trying to convince landlords that they were buying a good product – something that people would be able to comment on afterwards, not only for its taste, but also its 'body.' A favourite Merrydown legend credits a regular customer at a small village pub, known simply as 'Old Bert', for getting the new product on the road – or off the road and into the pubs of Sussex, Kent and London. Old Bert's local was Ian Howie's last call of a dispiriting day; no one, it seemed, was even prepared to sample the new cider; perhaps his face reflected how he was feeling, for the landlord at least listened to him. "Yes." – He said, he might be interested. He had a small cider drinking clientele – one of whom just happened to be sitting in the public bar at that time. "Let Old Bert try it," he suggested, and Ian put the sampling barrel on the counter.

Old Bert agreed to try half a pint – it was free after all – and took his time over it as Ian nervously awaited his verdict.

"Urr – Aah – Umps" – grunted old Bert, as he supped it down; but finally he returned the glass with a shake of his head – "Not enough go in it!" he said, damningly.

Ian, crestfallen, went out leaving the sampling barrel and taking with him the landlord's sympathies. Several days later, that same landlord was urgently placing an order for six barrels. Old Bert, it transpired, had drunk a further two pints of Merrydown cider that evening and had to be carried home for the first time in more than fifty years. The story had spread around the countryside and suddenly everyone was wanting to drink this 'new fangled cider' – so it was wherever Merrydown was tried.

With the headquarters of Merrydown long and well established since its arrival at Horam in 1947 – this success story now speaks for itself. Certainly, in this book, that is all I can put; but in their own book – 'Merrydown,' Forty Vintage Years,' by Graeme Wright – there is a lot more to delight the reader.

As far as Horam is concerned, there is another story to come from that beautiful part of Sussex, which in a way has something to do with my uncle's visit there. During that day in 1947 – after they had completed their business – Uncle Charles and his friends retired to the local pub for 'one or two' for the road, before returning to Brighton. Whilst in the pub, a conversation was struck up with some of the locals and the subject eventually turned to 'war yarns' – as was often the case such a short time after the hostilities had ended. During that conversation one of the locals told them that a man who lived close to Horam, who had been captured and made a prisoner of war, had taken his pet kestrel with him, kept it alive all through the years of captivity, and brought it back home with him when he had been liberated.

It was Uncle Charles who had told father and me this story, and I remember it had particularly intrigued me, and stuck in my mind for quite a long time afterwards, but as the years passed I completely forgot about it.

Recently, some forty two years after first hearing about this amazing relationship between man and bird – and during the time of writing this book, a coincidence occurred that I feel I should write here. The only thing that this story has to do with the year 1947 is that this is when I first heard about this man and his bird, and that that was also the year when – with the bird still alive – they went abroad yet again; this time to Africa.

I was browsing about in my local library, when I picked up a book I had never heard of before – one I had missed. It was called 'The Lure of the Falcon' – by Gerald Summers. The book

143

was mainly about the author, who lived at Horam, and his 'tamed' kestrel. It tells of their going to war together, being captured and both of them returning home safely at the end of the war. This immediately reminded me of the story I had heard all that time ago – an iota of time from the past had suddenly come back to me. I immediately set about trying to contact Gerald Summers, and after a lot of searching, contacted him at his Welsh home. He gave me his blessing to write about what happened – so here briefly is the story of Gerald Summers and the kestrel – 'Cressida.'

As a young boy growing up in the Sussex countryside, at a house called Old Acres, near Horam, Gerald had always had a very close affinity with nature and animals – particularly birds of prey and dogs. These interests had been kept up – indeed gathered in momentum during his years at the various schools he had attended, which included Rottingdean School, Bradfield and Gordonstoun.

In 1939, he joined the army, and in 1942, after various postings in the UK, he was posted to Folkstone – and from there on to Camber Sands near Rye in Sussex. Whilst he was there, Gerald decided that this was the right time and place for his beloved Lurcher bitch, 'Bracken' to join him – she was being looked after, in the meantime, at 'Old Acres.' One day, whilst exercising Bracken on the sands at Camber, the lurcher raced on ahead until out of sight behind a sand dune, Gerald says in his book – "I quickly joined Bracken and knelt beside her; there, her blue-black eyes glaring fear and defiance, her hooked beak open in threat, and one wing trailing limply beside her, was a little female kestrel. As I moved to pick her up, quick as light she flung herself on her back and grabbed my hand with needle sharp claws." – He took the kestrel back to where he was billeted – causing much interest in his unit. The bird had an injured wing, which was eventually, successfully put to rights. Over the weeks and months to come, the bird, which had been named Cressida, the lurcher, Bracken, and Gerald, became an inseparable trio – that is when it was possible to be together, there was after all a war going on, and they were in the process of doing some very intensive training. Eventually, came the day when the unit set sail for overseas duty.

Bracken, of course couldn't go with Gerald and remained back at Old Acres; but he felt he had no option but to give the bird its freedom or take it with him. He chose the latter, but whilst they were on the ship – 'The Derbyshire' – which had left port on Christmas Eve 1942, and with the shore still in sight, he writes – "on a sudden impulse I cut through her jesses with the penknife I always carried. I put her on the ship's rail facing the land and walked away without looking back; I couldn't bear to see her leave. I heard her calling, but kept on walking. I had to climb over some obstruction on the deck, and glanced back. Cressida, had already come half the distance between us; I held up my gloved fist and she glided onto it, at once lifting one of her feet and tucking it into her breast feathers – a sure sign of contentment. My conscience was clear and together we went below."

The ship took them to Algiers. When they had got settled there – and before going into battle – he took Cressida for long exploratory walks; the country was flat and he flew Cressida many times. The place was also a kestrel gourmet's paradise, with a large variety of insects making many succulent meals for her. There were hazards however, in the shape of other birds of prey, of which there were plenty – one large falcon nearly being the end of Cressida! When they eventually went into battle, he carried her everywhere inside his battle dress tunic – a procedure she accepted without protest. Here, she would lie down with her feet thrust in front of her and sleep like a puppy, unaware of what might be going on around her! In battle Cressida was quite disdainful of artillery fire – and not unduly worried about rifle or Bren-guns. During one ferocious battle, with machine gun fire whizzing overhead, Gerald suddenly remembered Cressida and a glance at the bolder she had chosen to perch on showed she still sat there – steady and unruffled, as imperturbable as the Tower of London! "– As I watched, a burst of machine gun bullets

145

skimmed by her side to rip open a large cactus, just above and behind her; she lowered her head slightly – as little concerned as if she had been mobbed by our local mistle thrushes at home."

Gerald was wounded in this battle – during which Cressida did disappear for a while, but was found later that night after he – despite his wounds – had searched long and desperately for her. A little later, whilst trying to find his unit, he was captured by the Germans. The German doctor who attended Gerald's wounds, turned out to be an amateur naturalist and a practising falconer. In fact, probably the only practising falconer in the German Medical Corps in North Africa – truly the ways of destiny are strange and wonderful – he was allowed to keep the bird with him.

Cressida remained with Gerald when he escaped from POW camp in Sicily, where he was eventually taken. He was recaptured after being hunted by dogs. Sometime later they were transferred to Italy and then to Stalag 18B at Muhlberg on Elbe in North Germany. They finally ended up in a camp in Czechoslovakia – after they had had one more unsuccessful escape attempt with more amazing adventures. They were eventually liberated by the Americans, and soon flown back to England – quite an adventure after nearly two and a half years for both man and bird – with Cressida now about four years of age.

Eventually, looking from the train from Victoria station on their way home, they saw that the names on the familiar stations such as Eridge, Mayfield and Heathfield had been blacked out – wartime measures taken in case of invasion to 'confuse' the enemy! They arrived at Horam and finally – in Gerald's words – "I took Cressida from her perch on the luggage rack and stepped out onto the platform; I had just begun my walk towards the barrier when I was almost overwhelmed by a hairy whirlwind. 'Bracken' had covered the length of the platform in a few elastic bounds; she was all over me, kissing me, leaping up to my chest and entwining herself around my legs – a welcome home to remember!"

146

This was the end of Cressida's adventures abroad for the time being, but in 1947 – after the trio had spent many unforgettable months together, Gerald decided he would try a career in agriculture in Africa – once again taking Cressida with him. That though, is another story and can be read in his book 'Where Vultures Fly.'

I now make a point of keeping in touch with Gerald; in a way, we are kindred spirits, but his affinity with furred and feathered creatures is something very special.

With only a week to go of the summer holidays, I crammed everything I could into what time remained, and I remember those final days before the new term as golden days. There was however, still the same 'blot on the landscape' – or, to be more precise – something that most people had become extremely wary of. It had been hoped that we might start seeing signs of an end to the infantile paralysis epidemic; it was thought that as the weather became cooler from September onwards, that this might lessen the numbers of people going down with the disease. For some reason many people associated the 1947 outbreak with the exceptionally hot weather, and the swimming pools and cinemas, had lost a lot of trade because people were avoiding such crowded areas where the disease was more likely to spread from, hoped desperately that they would soon see the end of this 'crippling' epidemic – but this was not to be. On September 13th in The Argus, under the heading – '662 New Cases of Infantile Paralysis,' the article went on to say – 'The Ministry of Health announced today, there were 662 notifications of infantile paralysis in England and Wales during last week – the highest weekly figure yet recorded, and fifty more than the previous week.' In another article about the disease on the same page, it said the champion British girl swimmer, Nancy Riach, who was competing in the European swimming championships at Monte Carlo, was suffering from the disease. A British official accompanying the team, said, it was improbable she would ever be able to take part in competitive events again!

147

Uncle Jimmy, now nearing the end of his seasonal job at Black Rock Pool, said that after this and various other announcements in the papers about the disease, the attendance numbers at the pool had plummeted again, after a brief period when the daily numbers had risen. My friends and I left the pool well alone, and carried on using the beaches – as, so it seemed, did everyone else who wanted to swim, whilst the hot weather continued.

Also, on Saturday September 13th Uncle Charles, Aunt Daphne and my two young cousins – Charles junior and Paul, arrived at number forty seven in their old Morris car. They stopped only long enough to pick me up, and after they said a quick hello to father and Sylvia, we started out on an enjoyable ride to Drusilla's – a small zoo and tea house – at Berwick, not far from Alfriston. We travelled the country roads via Lewes, admiring the magnificent downland views until arriving at our destination. Unlike so many places, Drusilla's hadn't closed down during the war years, and although the animals had gone from there for that period of time, the tearoom and the children's playgrounds remained open – difficult, during times of rationing and only a few cars qualifying for petrol coupons.

Drusilla's hadn't started off this way back in the1920's, when the tearooms had first opened. During that decade, Douglas Ann and his wife Drusilla had created a tearoom in the thatched cottage they had bought, not far from the banks of the Cuckmere River. They had started this, not just as a tearoom, but also – and mainly – to attract motorists from all over the south to show off their cars at a 'set' meeting place, on trips out into the country. A meeting place, it certainly became – in fact, it became the motoring showplace of the south. In the early thirties, Douglas Ann and Drusilla had agreed that their marriage was at an end. Although Drusilla herself left the scene at this stage – the name 'Drusilla's' had become so well known to so many motorists – it stuck! In 1934, Douglas Ann married for the second time; his new wife, Elizabeth, making up a partnership that would last for life. She played a very active part in the running of the 'now well known' tearooms and place where motorists could have a 'get together.' It was also Elizabeth who first thought of bringing animals there as an added attraction – "after all" she said, "the motorists often bring their children with them and they're not very interested in our just standing there talking about cars, so let's give them something to look at – and what could be better than animals?" This is how, in the 1930's, Drusilla's also became a 'baby' zoo – as Michael Ann, Elizabeth and Douglas's son, described it to me at a recent meeting.

In a 'rare' old brochure for Drusilla's, it says that, 'At the kiddies' corner, there are a large variety of things the kids can get up to – with pedal cars, rocking horses, 'toboggan' run, seesaws and swings.' For the grown ups – when they weren't showing off their cars – there was putting, archery and even a ballroom for evening dances – Drusilla's had their own dance band! There was also a miniature railway, which was described as – 'a thrilling circular run through the Sussex meadows, with signals, level crossings and a tunnel.' For a time this miniature train ran down to the nearby banks of the peaceful Cuckmere – where punts and canoes were available to hire for a pleasant hour or so on the river. You could easily get from here to the beach at Cuckmere Haven – a beautiful journey through the Sussex meadows.

Whilst we were there that afternoon, we looked at the animals, which included 'Joey' a kangaroo that was prone to escaping from time to time, causing some mayhem for those trying to recapture him – perhaps in someone's back garden. There was also a parrot which had a very wide vocabulary, which we found hilarious – at least Uncle Charles and I did. There was also a Rhesus monkey called Bill, a Drill monkey called Pedro, a Sooty Manatee called Sarah, and a Marmoset – who's name escapes me. There were various other small animals apart from these. We had all had an enjoyable day, one to remember, and I had learnt a bit more about the Sussex countryside – something that was to be very important to me later in life. Drusilla's is still going strong, and develops even more as the years go by – helped of course by the general public's enthusiasm for such places increasing all the time – the tearooms are still there as well.

The day after we went to Drusilla's, I went on a boat trip with two friends from the square – Timmy Martinez and Tony Morton, who was the owner of a small boat with an outboard motor, which was sturdy enough for rides – not too far from the shore. He usually only used the boat when the sea was 'millpond' calm or nearly so, and never much more than a mile from the beaches. When we left off from the Banjo Groyne there was only a light breeze prevailing, but by the time we were off Ovingdean, the wind had got up considerably and the sea was decidedly choppy. Tony decided to head inshore, aiming for a beach just below the corporation café on the undercliff walk at Ovingdean Gap. When we were just over a hundred yards from the beach, the engine stopped and Tony said – "well that's packed up then, I'll have to row it in, and to lighten it up a bit, you two can swim ashore!" We didn't mind this at all, but as we dived off the boat I noticed that Tony had a grin on his face. After we'd swum about halfway to the shore, we heard the outboard motor start up again, and a minute or two later, Tony – laughing his head off – passed us by and took the boat to the beach.

"For that," Timmy said, "you can buy the ice creams!"

The wind didn't get up any more, so we decided to return to the Banjo Groyne, keeping only about two hundred yards from the shore. The sea was still quite choppy, and small waves 'slapped' the bows, now and again splashing us – but we were never in any danger. The water was green – almost transparent, and you could see the rocks clearly in the depths below – the same rocks I often used to prawn around, and hoped to do so just once more before going back to school – There were only four 'full' days of the holidays left.

150

Sylvia paddling – Father fishing – Barcombe Mills, 1947

Horam Manor – which became the Headquarters of Merry Downe 1947 – A story of achievement
Aerial photograph taken from 'Mosquito' on sortie by
Squadron Leader Michael Wareham AFC, DFC

Gerald Summers with Cressida

Prisoners of War at Lattindens Farm, near Battle 1947
Left to Right – P.O.W. (name unknown) – Timmy – Farm worker

Audrey O'Neill with baby Valerie – outside the 'Hut' 1947

Drusilla's Tea Cottage – 1947

The Railway at Drusilla's – 'Deep in the Sussex Countryside'

Fishing boats at Hastings – 'Many years ago'

A catch – on 'The Hard' Brighton Seafront

Chapter Nine

**Hastings fishermen – A letter from East Sussex.
A school climbs back.**

Three days before returning to school, my Uncle Nat arrived at Sussex Square, " – Just passing through and thought I'd say hello." He said. Strictly speaking, Commander Nat Vaughan-Oliver, recently retired from the Royal Navy after wartime service, and now trying to write for a living, was no longer my uncle – he had divorced my Aunt Daphne in early wartime. The divorce had been an 'amicable' one, and in any case he'd been a friend of my father's for a lot longer than the marriage – so to me he would always be 'Uncle.' After he had told us all about what he had been doing since leaving the navy – which included having his converted houseboat moored on the River Adur, not far from Bramber – "perhaps something more than just a temporary home"- he said; he told us that he was on his way to Hastings that day to 'possibly' buy a boat from someone he knew slightly. He had decided that instead of moving his houseboat about from place to place, he would keep it moored somewhere close to where it was now, and buy another sturdily built boat of about 14ft.- 16ft. which he would use for trips up or down river or even out to sea from Shoreham Harbour; all in the quest of his favourite pastime – fishing! He and father had shared many pre-war days together, fishing the rivers and coastal areas of Sussex. He asked father, Sylvia and me if we'd like to go with him for a pleasant run to Hastings. They told him that they'd already made plans for that day, but I said that I'd gladly go with him. "Good," he said "we'll swap fishing yarns on the way, and I'll buy us a fish and chip lunch."

Half an hour later I climbed into the front passenger seat of his old 'Lanchester' motor car and we started on our way on the coast road to Hastings. On the way there we stopped at a place called 'The Buckle Inn' on the seafront just near Seaford – "a favourite old fishing haunt of your father's and mine," he told me. He went into the pub and had a drink with the landlord – whom he knew. I sat outside drinking a glass of ginger beer, and watched a large flock of seagulls gathering, not more than a hundred yards out to sea, where there was a shoal of mackerel – possibly feeding on white bait near the surface. After this we went through Eastbourne and on to Pevensey Bay, where Uncle Nat stopped to see another old acquaintance at a pub – and I was bought my second ginger beer of the morning. When we left off from here, we managed to make it all the way to Hastings without any further stops for refreshments! Uncle Nat drove to the old fishing area of the town, where he'd arranged to meet his 'friend' and hopefully buy the boat he'd come for. The fishermen's area of Hastings – a beautiful part of this old town, so steeped in fishing history, is known as 'The Stade'. I listened while Uncle Nat talked to some of the local fishermen; apparently they were getting good catches at that time, but although they were making a living from this harvest of the sea, they weren't netting the good dividends they deserved from their hard work – because of plummeting prices. The prices they were getting in 1947 were – a guinea a stone for soles, sixteen shillings a stone for plaice, and as low as 4/6 a stone for skate. Apart from the low prices at that time, the Hastings fishermen had been having a long running battle with the local council over the division of the beaches – in other words which beaches they had a right to and which beaches they didn't. This controversy has never been completely cleared up – or should I say made completely positive.

The year 1947 was to be an especially poignant one, as this is the year that the Hastings 'Deed of Compromise' became the law. In his book 'Fishermen of Hastings' – subtitled, '200 years of the

159

Hastings fishing community', the author, Steve Peak, has written about this new law in great detail. The Hastings Fishing Museum at Rock-a-Nore, which also stocks this book, is another place where one can find out more about Hastings fishing during the centuries. Briefly though, the 'Deed of Compromise of 1947' meant that the seafront at Hastings, the beaches that is, would be divided into three Stades – Stade is an old word for 'landing place'. This meant that the fishermen lost the right to use a lot of beach which they had previously used. They were allowed one of the three Stades – the 'blue' Stade which stretches from east of the lifeboat house and south of the miniature railway, to as far as you can go along the beach, in an easterly direction, to the cliffs. The council's reasons for this, or one of their reasons, was that they felt that the fishing industry at Hastings wasn't bringing anything into the town. What they wanted were more seaside attractions – the 'Deed of Compromise' made sure that they got these with the extra space. The fishermen could still fish of course – be it all – with a smaller fleet of boats and with less space for those that remained in operation. As I have said, there is still a lot of controversy about this, and although the names of the six original fishermen who agreed to sign this deed are recorded – no-one seems to know what authority they had at the time. The ceremony for the signing of the deed took place at the town hall on May 9th 1947. It was billed as a 'peace meeting' – but instead uproar broke out! However in the end the deed was signed, although a lot of the younger fishermen – the new generation – were very much against it.

On speaking to one of the fishermen recently, I was told that although the deed of compromise is complex – in a way, the ins and outs of it all suit them well enough for everything at present to be peaceful between the council and the fishing community. What I can't see, is how the council at that time failed to grasp that the Hastings fishing industry – which is the backbone of the town's history, and which has the largest 'off the beach' fishing fleet in the entire UK – was far more of a draw than the swings, roundabouts and boating pools. There are hundreds of ordinary seaside resorts, but only a few with as much character as Hastings. My wife and I and many other people we know who quite frequently visit the town, make a beeline for the old fishing quarter, where there is the added attraction of the fishermen's museum, which I'm glad to say, in this money grabbing age – is free of charge and open every day of the year apart from Christmas Day. Above all it is truly enjoyably atmospheric here – something of a bygone age which can still be seen today – something that should be treasured forever!

Uncle Nat bought his boat that day, and arranged to complete the deal a couple of weeks later. After this he went to speak to one of the lifeboat men he knew from before the war. The Hastings lifeboat of that time was called 'The Cyril and Lilian Bishop.' The boat had been built in 1930 at Cowes by J.Samuel White and Company. The cost of this new boat – the first Hastings lifeboat with an engine, was met from the legacy of a rich London woman, Mrs. Lilian Philpott. She had agreed while she was alive to finance two new lifeboats, on condition that one was named 'Cyril and Lilian Bishop,' after herself and her first husband. The boat arrived in Hastings on April 29th – 1931. In 1940, the Cyril and Lilian Bishop, took part in the historic Operation Dynamo – the rescue of the British expeditionary force and others, including French soldiers, from the beaches of Dunkirk – but that is another story! Whilst Uncle Nat was talking, I had a good look at this famous lifeboat; after this we went for a very late lunch of fish and chips at the 'Blue Saloon' café on the sea front – now called the 'Blue Dolphin.' Later that afternoon, after Uncle Nat had tied up a few loose ends, we returned to Brighton, taking the same roads back – this time only stopping at The White Horse at Rottingdean, just as they opened at six o'clock – where I had yet another ginger beer. A little later he dropped me off at Sussex Square, where, before saying our good-byes, he handed Sylvia some fresh plaice and soles; a very welcome gift – and for me, it had been another memorable day.

With Hastings still in mind, earlier in the book I put in most of a letter from 'M.P'. a Hastings lady who had had some rather 'horrific' experiences after moving to Hastings during the winter of 1947 – she was in the earlier stages of pregnancy then. In another letter, later on that year, things had improved somewhat – the brilliant summer of course, being one of the reasons. She writes:

"The awful winter was to be followed by a glorious summer, and as it warmed and the big thaw set in, out came the paint pots to brighten up shops, hotels and boarding houses, ready for what was hoped would be a flood of visitors. This optimism was justified as holiday makers were still quite happy with breaks in Britain, and people were glad to sit on beaches no longer festooned with barbed wire.

In those unsophisticated days, visitors were content with the entertainment's on offer; five cinemas, shows at The White Rock Pavilion, The Court Players on the pier, swimming galas at the bathing pool, Punch and Judy and Old Biddy paddling his tub round the waters edge. Apart from those staying in hotels and B & B's, there were the day trippers. These came in great convoys of buses from London and even further afield, at week-ends – and oddly, they all got dressed up for it. Men in their demob suits with collars and ties, women in ankle breaking heels and children in Sunday best. Having sat sweltering on a bus for up to three hours, they were deposited in the coach park in the fish market, and apart from the intrepid soul who asked the way to Woolworth's, they never moved more than fifty yards from where they were dropped off – so they didn't really see the best of Hastings.

Holiday-makers may have been good for the economy – landladies expected to make enough money in the summer to keep them all through the winter – but it made it virtually impossible to find permanent accommodation. In my case, my landlady decided to sell the house and all the tenants were turned out (no security of tenure then!). I'd taken temporary refuge in my mothers two rooms on the understanding that I could not stay there after the baby was born. I knew many others in the same situation, and every flat one saw advertised – stipulated 'NO CHILDREN.' Despite the fact that it seemed to be a crime to have a family, it was a boom year for babies. This is how maternity care was in 1947 – just pre the welfare state:

'Providing you had no facilities for a home birth, there were two options – both of which had to be paid for. One was a nursing home, which I couldn't afford, and the other was the hospital – known as the 'muni.' – which had previously been the workhouse. I can't remember the exact fee, but I think it was a little over £5 – half to be paid before you went in, and the other half after the birth – it was like having your baby C.O.D. I recall that I paid the second half at 2/6d per week. It was quite a sum in those days when the wage for an unskilled male worker was around £4 per week, and a female clerical worker got £2-15s.

There was an anti-natal clinic on Tuesdays. The waiting area was a long corridor, furnished with an assortment of chairs and sofas covered in brown mock leather, which I believe was called Rexine and which got very hot indeed as the sun blazed in through the windows, which lined the entire length of one side. It was quite funny when we moved up a place – there was a loud 'ripping' noise as we peeled off one seat to a sound like dozens of whoopee cushions, as we settled on the next one.

The examination room had 4 or 5 cubicles, with curtains which were never drawn – so a good view was had by all. Modesty and dignity were foreign words – no one had learned the language – it was a world away from the care mothers get today. The examination was somewhat cursory, so much so that when I went in one Tuesday and mentioned that I'd had pain for 12 hours, I was told to come back next week. Actually I was back in three hours and had my daughter half an hour later! Unfortunately

163

there were a lot of other births that evening, and we ended up in beds so close together that we could have all held hands with the greatest of ease – it must have looked like a field hospital. We were later shunted to other parts of the hospital and I ended up in a children's ward. They were all severely disabled, and most of them had been abandoned at birth – so never had any visitors. I wonder what became of them all?

My hospital stay lasted ten days, after which I was rescued by my grandmother, where I stayed for six weeks, until we found a home in Hastings. My husband left Maidstone where he had been working and lodging, he got a job here in a girls school as a cook/ dogs body, and the three of us settled into two attic rooms overlooking Alexandra Park; our rent was £1.10s. per week plus 1s for laundry and 6d. per bath. Water had to be fetched in a bucket from a tap in the toilet on the floor below. The landlady and her son had the ground floor, and the other two storeys were shared by nine adults and three children, with one bath and one toilet between us. The sloping ceiling by our dormer window was a bit of a hazard, and my husband hit his head so many times, that I wonder he didn't suffer brain damage!

Despite the drawbacks, we were all as happy as sand boys – having a roof over our heads, and there were also compensations. We could watch the weekly firework displays in the park from our window; I could bump my pram down three flights of stairs and sit in the park practically every day during that wonderful summer and autumn. I won't forget Hastings in 1947. Some of it was dire, but there were a lot of good things to remember – the good old trolley buses which were quiet, clean and punctual; the friends I made, and the sharing of what little we had. Maybe the reason we were happy was because we didn't necessarily expect to have what we wanted, but contented ourselves with what we needed!"

Thursday the eighteenth of September 1947, was certainly a bittersweet day for me; not only was it the last full day of my summer holiday before returning to school, but also this was another very special day for Jill. A few weeks earlier, Miss. Rita Williams, the Lttlehampton beauty queen, had issued a much publicised challenge to Jill and other Sussex Beauty Queens – including Miss. Peggy O'Neill who was Miss. Chichester, Cynthia Lynch who was Miss. Eastbourne and June Pooley who was the Beauty Queen of Hove – to see who would become the outright Beauty Queen of Sussex. It had been agreed that this special contest would be held on the evening of September 18th at the 'Pavilion-in-the-Green,' Littlehampton. As this was my last day, Jill realised I couldn't go to see the event – nor could father or Sylvia, but we assured her our thought would be with her.

I spent my last day of 'freedom' by cramming as much as I could into the hours left to me. I remember father saying to me – "you're acting like a condemned man!" – to which, I replied – "Well–?"

Most of my friends had by now gone back to their particular schools, so I decided to go to the YMCA in Old Steine and play myself at snooker. When I got there, however, I saw someone I knew slightly, and we played table tennis. I was thoroughly trounced by this acquaintance – called Brian Leach. He was the son of a local publican, who had long been associated with the Brighton fishing industry. After we left the YMCA, we went for a walk down to what is known as The Fisherman's Hard – this is by the beaches, between the two piers and where the fishing boats used to come into beach, even selling some of their fish here. I always remember keenly watching one particular man who used to fillet fish here at lightning speed. Brian introduced me to some of the fishermen he knew; I also saw closely for the first time the two new Brighton pleasure boats – 'The Alexander' and 'The Montgomery' – named of course, after those two famous generals of World War II. Both of these boats had only recently been built at Shoreham. Brian managed to get us a free trip on the Montgomery, which was very enjoyable, except that when we got

165

a reasonable way from the beach, it started to pour with rain – I remember the boatman saying, "it looks like the summer's coming to an end at last – shouldn't be surprised to hear some thunder!"

About these boats; in an article in 'The Motor Boat & Yachting' it says – "– Continuity of employment is a good thing for both men and boats, thinks Major Hill, (local boat entrepreneur) – and surely he is right. Acting on this opinion, he has arranged that the two fifty four seater passenger craft which he has had built for service at Brighton, shall be employed during the winter months in inshore trawling. The crews – three men to each boat – will have the opportunity of keeping permanent jobs and the craft will be earning money nearly all the year round."

Another boat built for similar use to The Alexander and The Montgomery, was the 'Martha Gunn' – this was forty seven foot long – the others thirty nine foot – and could carry sixty five passengers. In the years to come these boats became a familiar part of the Brighton seafront scene – and 'old friends' to many trippers.

I was going to go to Brighton races in the afternoon, but with no-one to go with and as it was still raining from time to time, I decided to go to the pictures instead. I went to The Regent cinema and saw 'Captain Boycott' with Stewart Grainger – and Cecil Parker in the title role. Later on I met Aunt Daphne outside The Hippodrome; she had got us seats to see the Ralph Reader gang show – 'The Gang's All Here.' We enjoyed the show very much, and before we said our good-byes, Aunt Daphne reminded me that Uncle Charles would pick us up at three o'clock the following afternoon, for the trip back to college.

On arriving back home, at just after ten thirty p.m. that evening, I found that Sylvia and father were 'raising a glass' in celebration – they had just had a phone call from Jill saying she was now 'Miss. Sussex' – she had won that evening's contest at Littlehampton. I joined them in toasting my sister with a glass of cider, and soon after this went to bed and instant sleep – it had

166

been an odd sort of a day – during which I had been constantly aware that the next day I would be back at school, and sleeping in yet another strange bed.

I had a late breakfast that morning, and although Jill had come home very late after her triumph of the night before, she had got up before me, and I now found myself the only male in Sussex to be sharing a breakfast table with 'the most beautiful girl in the county!' Jill told me a lot of what had happened the previous evening, and also said that the whole thing had been well covered by the press, and I would be able to read more about it that day – she had forgotten I was due back at Lancing before The Argus would be on the streets. However, there was a report in The Sussex Daily News – of which, father had bought four copies, and I did see reports in other local papers later on. In one paper, under the headline, 'Jill is most beautiful girl in Sussex' it went on with a smaller headline which said – 'Brighton Has Counties Best Beauty Queen' – and continued to say 'Miss. Jill Knowles, Brightons Beauty Queen became Miss. Sussex 1947, when she was given first place at 'The Battle of the Sussex Beauties' at the Littlehampton Pavilion-in-the-Green last night. Said Jill, "I am proud to be the first Miss. Sussex and I hope I shall give the county some useful publicity."

Jill received a silver cup presented by Mr. Will Hammer. As a result of her success, Jill will be given a screen test with a view to appearing in a film being produced by Hammer enterprises. After the contest, Mr. Hammer commented that no better array of beauties could be seen in any part of England!

I remember father saying to me after learning of Jill's victory at Littlehampton, that when he and mother had driven back from Climping on our many pre-war visits to the beaches there, and stopped in the town for a drink before continuing on our journey, they sometimes passed by The Pavilion-in-the-Green, and no-one could have guessed what the future had in store, at that particular venue, for the little girl sitting in the back of the car.

During that last morning, I went on one of my walks to Ovingdean, coming back via Ovingdean Gap on the 'Overcliff Walk.' I had passed by the 'Art Decor' style building of St. Dunstans – during the war years the St. Dunstaners had been evacuated to Church Stretton in the hills of Shropshire. They had returned to Ovingdean in 1946. Some St. Dunstaners had also played a very active part in the war. In, 'St. Dunstans a story of accomplishment':- it says, "many St. Dunstaners themselves worked in civil defence as air raid wardens, roof spotters identifying aircraft by sound, and in the home guard.

I continued my walk past Roedean school – both this famous school and St. Dunstans had been taken over by HMS Vernon during the war years – the girls from Roedean being evacuated to Keswick in the north of England. What is not widely known is that Roedean school began as a school in Sussex Square.

On the subject of girls schools, people in the square, having noticed that repair building work was going on at number twenty two – the part of St. Mary's Hall School for Girls called St. Nicholas House – wondered when the girls would be back in residence again. In my book 'The Tree Climbers,' I told how, while I was attending the kindergarten there, and Jill, the girls school – the oldest school in Brighton and possibly the oldest girls school in England – it had had to close down in 1940. At that time, there was the very real threat of invasion, and as the school didn't have the funds to evacuate, the parents were asked whether they wanted to keep their children where they were, or send them to other schools. The choice had been to send the girls to other schools, and consequently the school had closed forthwith

Now, Babington House at no's 2 and 3 Chichester Terrace, had re-opened and the aim was that the main school on the Eastern Road, which, during one period of the war had been occupied by The Lake Superior Regiment from Canada – as had St.Nicholas House, would re-open in the not too distant future, but there was plenty of work to be done there yet.

By early 1947, with work continuing at the main school, but the way ahead seeming to be clear, advertising took place to secure more pupils. A Thanksgiving service for the re-opening was held in St. Mark's Church on 22nd February 1947 – by then there were already nineteen boarders and forty one day girls in the school.

The enormous task of getting everything back in working order again is best described by using some excerpts from a letter written by Miss. Harriet Robinson, who had been appointed head mistress in July 1946 – she writes:

"– On Friday, September 19th 1946, we came into residence at the hall from Babington; Miss. Willis (secretary) Mrs. Cameron (cook/caterer) and Ethel Philipps (maid). Our first night here was a memorable one. The escape of gas was so bad in our bedrooms that we had to sleep in my study! Then, very tired and dirty, we thought how comforting a hot bath would be. To our dismay, though there was plenty of hot water, there was not a single bath-plug in the building. I had to go down to Babington to find one. In spite of difficulties, however, it was really thrilling to be at last living at the Hall, and to be occupying rooms vibrating and pulsing with memories of bygone days.

On looking back over the past year, my chief feeling is one of deep gratitude for all the help that has been given, for loyal, hard working staff in the school itself, in the kitchen, and in the garden. To these devoted workers the school owes very much. Then my thoughts turn in sincere thankfulness, to all helpers outside the school, and especially to Miss. Ghey and Miss. Galton."

To explain about Miss. Ghey and Miss. Galton I will add a piece which can be found on pages 34/35, of 'A Short History of St. Mary's Hall.'

"To the onlooker, progress towards re-opening appeared to be slow. This was certainly felt to be the case by the St. Mary's Hall Association who's president was Miss. Ghey. She and Miss. Galton at Blunt House, Oxted, their coaching establishment, had kept the St. Mary's Hall Association very much alive during the war. Regular meetings and fund raising activities had been held and now Miss. Ghey and many other friends of the school were becoming impatient for action of some sort. Miss. Ghey and Miss. Galton approached the Bishop of Chichester, as acting chairman of governors, who promised to enlist the help of the Diocese – Miss. Ghey for her part promised to begin an appeal to the St. Mary's Hall Association. The early response of promises of £3000 encouraged the governors to go ahead with plans for the re-opening, and by the autumn the sum of £5000 had been raised by the appeal. No help was forthcoming from the Diocese – not surprisingly, they just did not have the resources required."

In her letter, Miss. Robinson asks, "– and what of the future? We shall have reached the 200 mark when the main school re-opens in January 1948, and repairs to number twenty two Sussex Square began last week."

The outcome was that St. Nicholas House at 21/22 Sussex Square re-opened in 1948 under the new name – 'St. Hilary's House' – and by May 1949 there were 228 children in the school; 100 boarders, 128 day girls and a kindergarten. Hard work and determination in the face of grim reality had eventually won the day, and the school flourishes to this day.

When I eventually arrived home that morning, there was still over an hour before lunch time, so I decided to have a walk around both the bottom and top gardens in Sussex Square. When I got to the top gardens I immediately made my way to my favourite fir tree – a Monterey Cypress – in the top left corner. This tree had been the one that we children, during the wartime, had made our special tree – with a 'secret place' near to the top of it. I sat here for a while, remembering many of the incidents that happened in the gardens during those days of air raids and bombings and seemingly never ending summers. There were the good times and the bad times – but I have already told of all this in my book 'The Tree Climbers.' One incident that does come to mind however was when I was sitting at the top of the tree with

Timmy and a couple of the others, and we had tried to sling 'mud bombs' from our lofty position into a basement area, where someone we didn't like, lived. The 'mud bomb' that I had thrown, which was a particularly hard one, had been a bad shot and had gone clean through someone's window; resulting in my pocket money being stopped until the window was paid for – that was the first and last time we played that game!

I didn't eat much that lunch time – once again my nerves had started getting the better of me, and I felt annoyed with myself. I think that at that moment, if I had said to Sylvia – "look, I'm sorry, I just don't want to go back to school as a boarder – couldn't I please see if Brighton College would have me as a day boy?" – She would probably have said "yes" – without much hesitation; she understood how I felt and sympathised with me – but father would have been immovable, he had been set on my going to Lancing for a long time, and, of course, it had always been my mother's wish as well. I kept my feelings quiet from him, but whether he'd guessed that anything was 'amiss' with me, I could only guess at myself.

At just before three o'clock, Uncle Charles arrived – and shortly afterwards we began the journey to North Lancing. A little later, as we approached the old Toll Bridge at Shoreham, Lancing College Chapel loomed large in the familiar landscape. At this point, my nerves seemed to settle, and I started to look forward to seeing my new found friends of the previous term again – there would be much to talk about, and starting in a 'new house' was certainly going to be something of an adventure as well.

Chapter Ten

New term, new house – New Playhouse in Kemptown. New Year.

We arrived on the chapel quadrangle at Lancing at just before four o'clock; the afternoon had turned very humid, and we could see large banks of threatening storm clouds building up to the west of the college. By just before six o'clock all the parents had left to go home – the parents of the new boys, being the last to leave off. Father and Sylvia had only stayed for half-an-hour – saying a brief hello to Mr. Chamberlin, and then taking their leave. The bell for chapel rang out sharp at six o'clock, for our first service of the term. Later, during the evening, we swapped yarns about what we'd done on our holidays, and also, remembering our own feelings when we were new boys the previous term, we got to know the 'new' new boys, who all looked a bit homesick. At about eight o'clock there was a violent thunder storm – with bright flashes of lightning and deafeningly loud claps of thunder; this disturbed many of the boys, and reduced one of the new boys to putting his hands over his ears and eventually succumbing to tears; we felt sorry for him – as did one of the new house captains, Armstrong, who did his best to comfort him.

Mr. Chamberlin talked to the whole house at prayers that evening – house prayers were usually only held on Sunday evenings, but this was a special occasion – he introduced us to the head of Teme House, Anthony Moncrieff, and the other house captains. He told us what he expected of us, and then wished us all goodnight – remembering the Christian names of every boy, including the new boys. I found myself in the junior dormitory –

the dormitories were smaller than they had been in Heads House. I felt no home sickness at all, and wondered what I had been worrying about. One thing I did know though, was that I would still sooner have been a day boy and able to go home each night, rather than be a boarder!

The next morning we started to settle into the routine of things again, and ahead of us stretched all the days of term right up to the 19th of December – ninety long days away – a very different feeling to that memorable first day of the summer holidays.

During the first days of the term, I got quite a few remarks about my sister, after her latest triumph in the Beauty Queen stakes. There were plenty of questions for me, such as – "when's your sister visiting you again Knowles?" Or – "Is it true your sister's going to be a film star?" – One question that threw me though, was – "Is your sister going to start wearing shorter skirts Knowles?" This speculation had come to be, because of a newspaper report on the 25th September, which had been headlined – 'Ministers Join Battle of the Skirt' – "Shorter the better!" said Sir Stafford Cripps – the president of the Board of Trade; he was trying to put a stop to the alarming amount of material being used for the 'New Look' with it's extra long skirts, during a time when materials were in extremely short supply. The Guild of Creative Designers were in any case trying to find a compromise between the 'exaggerated fashions' that Paris was trying to force upon the world, and the existing fashions. Mr. Belcher, the parliamentary secretary, also had his views on this subject – and said, "I would like to see them still shorter, I have no wish at all that they should create indecent designs, but I think they might slice off a little more." A compromise was eventually reached, and before long – at school – the subject of my sister and her Beauty Queen competitions and the talk about ladies skirts, only rarely entered our everyday conversations.

In the college, on the floor below the dining hall, there is an armoury, where our uniforms for the 'Corps,' C.C.F. or

173

Combined Cadet Force, to give it its full title, were kept in small square lockers, and the rifles neatly placed in numbered circular racks built around the supporting pillars of this large hall – woe betide the boy who didn't keep his rifle well oiled, and spotlessly clean! On the wall outside the armoury, was the only public telephone, for the boys use, in the school – surprisingly, in those days I can never remember there being a queue to use this pay phone. I used to phone home once a week from here, usually keeping the conversation to three or four minutes, but I could have had longer if I'd wanted, and all for the same price. For local calls, which cost three pence per call, there was no limit to the amount of time you had.

My call back home on Friday 3rd October was certainly one of the longer ones – I was expecting it to be. This was the day that Winston Churchill received the 'Freedom of the Borough of Brighton' – and I knew that because of father's deep respect for the man, he would certainly have tried to see some of the proceedings. He told me that he and Sylvia had been amongst the crowds when Mr. Churchill was driven to The Royal Pavilion, and they did get quite a good view of him for a few moments before the crowds became too much, and they returned home. In The Argus that night the main story said, "– Dressed in morning suit and wearing a typical Churchillian top hat, Mr. Winston Churchill received a roaring welcome from the people of Brighton today. Thousands lined the route, when at mid-day he drove from The Hotel Metropole to The Royal Pavilion grounds to be guest of honour at a luncheon in The Corn Exchange. Mr. Churchill rode sitting on the hood of a large touring car. Looking very fit and smiling broadly he acknowledged the cheers of the crowd with his famous V sign and a wave with his topper.

Crowds poured into Brighton this morning hours before Mr. Churchill was due to receive The Freedom of the Borough." The article went on to say – "After Mr. Churchill had driven from the hotel to The Pavilion, enormous crowds gathered outside the

174

south gate. They blocked North Street – traffic was diverted and stretched to the sea front. Mr. Churchill was received by the Lord Lieutenant of Sussex (Lord Leconfield) and the Mayor and Mayoress of Brighton (Alderman and Mrs. T.E. Morris)." The visit was a huge success – a piece of Brighton history.

Teme House, as a new house under the guidance of Mr. Chamberlin, had got off to a very good start, and by mid October, new house 'societies' had started to take shape; one of these was the play reading society. This was held on many of the Saturday evenings during the Christmas and Lent terms, when the cinematograph society wasn't showing a film in the great hall. Just about the whole house would cram into Mr. Chamberlin's sitting room/study on these evenings – the 'cast' having already been chosen, and everyone else an audience of listeners. We read such plays as 'Flare Path' by Terence Rattigan, 'Thark' – the Haunted House and many others of a similar light vein. I used to enjoy these evenings very much, as did everyone else – something of Lancing I shall always remember.

On one of the Sundays in October Mr. Chamberlin took a small group of us for tea at a special teahouse he knew well at Steyning. It was a beautiful late Autumn day and before we had tea, we climbed to the top of Chanctonbury Ring and admired the astonishing views from there – on a clear day you can see several counties. I found this a strange yet exhilarating place, and remembered the stories I had heard about it when the Romans had been here, so many centuries ago. It is thought they used the top of Chanctonbury Ring as a place of worship, and that a small chapel had been built near the summit. We spent half an hour up here – and then ran all the way down to the bottom, where we waited for Mr. Chamberlin to catch up. The tearooms we went to were in the High Street and, quite simply, called 'The Steyning Tea Rooms.' There was a low, beamed ceiling, and inside, it was just as one would imagine an old fashioned teahouse to look like – there was a tea garden as well. Similar to last term, when we had gone with

Mr. Chamberlin to a Tudor style tearoom at North Lancing, the rationing situation didn't seem to count much here, and there was a good selection of home-made cakes to go with the toast and butter. We arrived back at college, well in time for chapel.

During the early days of October, there were reports that the numbers of cases of infantile paralysis in the county were decreasing, and on Saturday 11th October it was reported that the numbers had dropped to 402 cases throughout the United Kingdom; this of course was still a lot – but the signs were optimistic and everyone hoped that we would soon see the end of this epidemic. At the beginning of the term the school had been saddened to hear of the death of one of the boys – David Walmsley – from this disease. I remember him from the summer term, when, as a house captain on 'duty' in the tea hall one afternoon, he helped some of us juniors to get tea out of a practically empty urn, by tilting it for us – we would normally have been left to our own devices! He was a kind and helpful person.

Remembering the world news – also on October 11th there was a report that – 'a full house of delegates was expected to cram into the UN chamber in New York, to hear the United States announce its long awaited policy on Palestine, in the shadow of reported Arab threats of war.' The outcome of this history making 'event' was that partition of the Jews and Arabs was agreed upon – and the year 1948 would see the birth of the new State of Israel.

The sport that term was mainly football – there was no rugger played at Lancing then. There were also squash, five's and cross country running. Lancing is well known for its five mile cross country run – a bit more than five miles actually – with the last mile made more difficult by having to wade through a number of dykes, even if there was ice on them. I enjoyed this as much as the football; particularly liking the undulating downland we ran over – leaving off from near the sanitarium and finishing up at the last dyke near the Sussex Pad Hotel.

176

There were several Saint's day's during that term, but as Mr. Chamberlin didn't encourage boys who lived nearby, as I did, to go home on them, I would usually go into Worthing with some of my friends. We usually went to the cinema, then a café and then make sure we got the bus back in time for evening chapel. In those days there were several cinemas in Worthing, including The Rivoli, The Dome, The Odeon and The Plaza. On one of our outings there we took two of the new boys with us and saw 'How Green Was My Valley' at The Dome. I remember that a play called 'The Poltergeist' was showing at The Connaught Theatre – brought to the stage by 'The Overture Repertory Players,' – I wished that I had been able to see this, but that would have been impossible during term time. I much preferred 'live' theatre to the cinema. I particularly used to like the ones put on at Brighton College, just before Christmas each year – they were of a high standard and very enjoyable.

My sister had also got strong leanings towards the theatre, and I had been pleased to learn on a phone call to home a week beforehand, that she had joined a new repertory company at the old 'Kings Cliff' cinema in Sudeley Place, Kemptown. The papers had called it 'The Metro Cinema' but we still called it by its old name, and now it was to be called 'The Playhouse.' The new company she had joined called itself Playhouse Productions, and their first play was due to open at the end of October – it was called, 'Viceroy Sarah.' This play, by Norman Ginsbury, is about the friendship between Queen Anne and The Duchess of Marlborough, and is based on fact. Jill's part in the play was as, Elizabeth, Lady Bridgewater – one of the daughters of the duchess. In the next year or so I would go to see several plays here; father and Sylvia went from time to time as well – usually dropping in for a drink at The Sudeley Arms nearby, during the interval.

On Wednesday 18th November, in the afternoon, I had to go to Shoreham for an overdue visit to the dentist. I remember that the

177

dentist I used to see during my years at Lancing was called 'Broadbridge' – Mr. Chamberlin told me that he was a lord, but never used the title. On that particular afternoon, before walking back over the toll bridge to the college, hopefully in time for tea, I bought a copy of the Evening Argus, and became worried after I had read the headline and what followed it – it said, 'BIG SOUTH COAST FIRE' – Princes Gate, block of luxury flats in King George V Avenue, Worthing, was partly destroyed by fire today. My grandparents had moved to King George V Avenue earlier in the year, and although I knew that they didn't live at these particular flats, I knew that they lived close by. On arriving back at school instead of hurrying to the tea hall, I went straight to the telephone by the armoury and phoned them up. I knew that they would have quite a bit to say because the article had gone on to say – "firemen from Worthing, Bognor, Hove, Lancing and Findon fought flames, which in an hour completely gutted the top tier of the flats. Seven families are homeless. The smoke was so dense that the firemen had to wear respirators." My grandmother answered the phone and told me that she and grandfather had heard all the noise and seen the comings and goings, but that was it – the papers obviously knew much more than they did. That week-end in The Worthing Herald it said that 18 families had been made homeless by fire, and a considerable time is likely to elapse before the families can return. I finished my conversation with my grandmother saying I hoped she and grandfather would be visiting Sussex Square sometime over Christmas – she assured me they would.

For sometime now the whole school had been 'geared up' to the biggest event of the year – the wedding of Princess Elizabeth to Prince Philip. We had been told, we would be able to listen to some of the radio coverage of this historic event. The big day, Thursday 20th November, duly arrived, and the wedding took place without a hitch. We heard everything very clearly, but as the papers pointed out afterwards, '– many of the brilliant assembly

178

of 2,500 in the lofty, pillared vastness of Westminster Abbey, saw nothing of the service. The huge congregation sitting by their wireless sets in all parts of the world heard more clearly than some sitting a few yards away.'

There were of course headlines in all the papers telling of the wedding – The Argus said, "A few minutes after Princess Elizabeth – now the Duchess of Edinburgh – had driven in the glass coach with her sailor/husband back to Buckingham Palace from her wedding, a solid mass of well wishers crying 'We want the bride!' surged to the palace railings. Thousands broke through the police cordons and dashed into the palace fore-court. Police and troops were helpless – and then, the happy bridal pair appeared on the balcony of the palace and waved repeatedly." At school, we listened as all this was vividly described to us – the BBC did a marvellous job in its presentation – it had been another special day to remember in 1947.

In early December I visited my grandparents in Worthing, and was disappointed to learn that as grandfather hadn't been too well lately, they wouldn't be coming to see us over Christmas, but promised to phone us on Christmas morning. When I left their flat that afternoon, I was £1 richer – an early Christmas present.

Of the two main news items that had been ongoing through 1947 – in India there was much violence, and Mr. Ghandi was on another hunger strike – causing much concern. The Palestine situation seemed to be resolved as far as partition was concerned, and the forthcoming new state of Israel was very much a part of everyday conversation. It would be interesting to see how things went in 1948 – but the hostilities between the Jews and the Arabs continued, and on December 7th it was announced that both sides were calling up their young men to fight.

On December 14th it was announced that Earl Baldwin of Bewdley had died – he was better known as Stanley Baldwin. He served as prime minister three times. In Angela Thirkell's book – 'Three Houses,' she tells of the Baldwin family and the Ridsdale

179

family and their connections with Rottingdean and 'Northend House' at Rottingdean. In the book she says – "Our mother's cousin, Stanley Baldwin, had married the elder Miss. Ridsdale and every year they came down from their home in Worcestershire to spend some weeks at Rottingdean."

The Ridsdales eventually moved to Lewes Crescent, which adjoins Sussex Square – that was in the 1920's. Julian Ridsdale, who I also remember quite well, was a friend of father's. Molly, Julian's daughter, still lives at Lewes Crescent – she became one of my mother's very good friends. Molly's brother – also called Julian, was an MP for thirty seven years and is now retired. Angela Thirkell, writes of their father Julian, "– He was always very kind and whenever we met him in town, he took us straight to a toy shop and bought us a toy." I remember him as a very kind man who always had time to speak to us children, and on one occasion, before the war and sweet rationing, he came into the kiosk near Sussex Square, and on seeing me in there, asked what I would like; I replied – "A sherbet dip please." – And he immediately bought me one.

At college, the term seemed to have gone by very quickly, and once again we looked forward to the holidays. On the last day of term, father and Sylvia came over by bus for the carol service – an important and very enjoyable part of the Lancing calendar. The festival of nine lessons and carols went very smoothly, with various boys and masters reading the lessons. This service started with the choir coming into the chapel in procession, singing 'Once in Royal David's City' – atmospheric beyond description, unforgettable! By the time the service was over it was nearly dark outside, and after saying goodbye to my friends, and of course, Mr. Chamberlin; father, Sylvia and I walked down to the bus stop near the Sussex Pad Hotel, where we caught the bus for Pool Valley, and then the town bus for home and the beginning of the Christmas holidays. After meeting many of my friends again, including Keith Denyer at number nineteen, arrangements started almost immediately for our own carol singing on Christmas Eve. We would sing around the square and crescents as we had done, more or less, since I could remember. During the war years, despite the black out, we never missed a Christmas Eve, and were expected and appreciated at many of the flats and houses we called at on our route. We always practiced before the big day arrived, and I remember that we all sang well and were often asked for encores – the Christmas of 1947 was to be no different.

My sister, Jill, in the meantime, still helped out at The Playhouse in Sudeley Place when she had the time, and also did some freelance modelling; but now she was busy rehearsing for the pantomime – 'Jack and the Beanstalk,' at The Grand Theatre in North Road, Brighton, which was due to start before Christmas, on Monday 22nd December. She and her friend Pat Rose – the daughter of the owner of the Grand Theatre, Albert Rose, both had small parts in this pantomime, which 'boasted' a large cast of well known names. It was brought to the Grand Theatre by Lupino Lane in association with Will Hammer and Albert Rose, and the cast of seventy performers included the world famous Lupino family; in the supporting cast and well down on the billing, were the names, Morecombe and Wise – their early days – Jill got to know them quite well. Father and Sylvia with a few others, including myself, were given tickets for the first performance; we enjoyed the evening enormously and Morecombe and Wise brought the house down!

On the twenty third of December, a report from India said that – 'The last Moslem Refugees from India, crossed into Pakistan during the week-end; they completed their journey without incident and were taken into refugee camps. They were lucky, for it is estimated that 400,000 people – both Moslem and Hindu – have been slaughtered since the partition of old India, while a further 100,000 have suffered cruelly from starvation and exposure. Official figures for today show that more than 8,500,000 refugees, almost equally divided between Hindu and Moslem, have crossed the Indo-Pakistan border in the last four months – the largest migration in history.'

On Christmas Eve, in the afternoon, I went to the pictures with Keith – we went to The Savoy cinema and saw 'Just William's Luck.' The carol singing began at six o'clock; the weather was kind to us, but colder weather was forecast after Christmas. The evening went well, it was nice to keep this tradition of ours alive.

On Christmas Day, in the early evening, we had our first Christmas Tree Party at number forty seven – this had also been a 'tradition' with us at number thirteen. Every Christmas night during the war years and before that, the room would be darkened, the candles on the tree lit and small presents handed down to the children – it was a magical time we specially looked forward to in our younger years. Now we were all a bit older, tea and Christmas cake and the lighting of the candles sufficed, and we were pleased that nearly all the faces we had seen over the years attended again – this time with the addition of Dickie and Kathleen Chalmers, and Keith's mother and father and brother David.

The day after Boxing Day, I called on Blanche, the little man who did odd jobs for us, and who, before the war, had been a gardener in Sussex Square gardens. I had, during the latter part of the war, when I was on one of my walks over the downs, been followed home by a stray dog – something like an Old English sheepdog, with a bit of something else added. I wasn't allowed to keep him, but Blanche took him in and had had him ever since. The agreement – seeing that I had found the dog – was that I could take him out for walks whenever I wanted to, they had named him Bobby. On that morning we walked to Ovingdean and back over the downs; on the way back we were followed by three aggressive looking dogs – probably strays – they had a mean and hungry look about them, and I feared for Bobby, who was extremely docile, so, putting him back on his lead, I ran the final half mile off the downs, with Bobby looking at me from time to time, panting hard and probably thinking that this was a most unusual type of walk he was having. However the dogs veered off when I got as far as the golf club, and that was the last that we saw of them.

Although the rationing still continued at the end of 1947, and would do for years to come, we seemed to have enough of everything. There had been plenty of imported fruit in the shops over Christmas, including oranges, bananas and grapes – 'luxuries' to us. Although there were more turkeys about than since before the war, we had stuck to our usual chicken – still something of a luxury to us at that time! The fuel situation was still a worry to everyone, but it wasn't as drastic as it had been – we just hoped that we wouldn't see another winter like the last one.

In The Argus on New Years Eve 1947, the main report said – 'Chaos on Icy Roads, Traffic Paralysed.' These had been familiar headlines the previous winter, and we began to fear the worst again – we needn't have worried, the winter to come would be nothing like that one!

Father, Sylvia and I accepted the Denyer's invitation again to go to their flat at number nineteen Sussex Square, for a small party on New Years Eve. Also at that party, this time, was Keith's oldest sister, Hazel (I secretly had a crush on her); his other sister, Heather, was married and living in Canada. We played charades again during an enjoyable evening – this time acting out words or names that had been in the news during 1947. For example, if it was a name we had chosen, and the name was 'Churchill' – we would act out one scene which had the word church in it, another scene with the word hill, and a final scene with the name Churchill. The audience had to guess the name. All extremely obvious of course, but good fun for us in becoming actors just for a while. We chose two words that evening to base our play-acting on – 'Snow-drift' and 'Heat-wave' – meaningful words at the end of the eventful year of 1947.

183

Winston Churchill arriving at Metropole Hotel, Brighton after receiving 'Freedom of the Borough'

CHANCTONBURY RING, SUSSEX.

Chanctonbury Ring

185

Jill wins Miss Sussex Title
Top left: Rita Williams (Miss Littlehampton);
Top right: Peggy O'Neill (Miss Chichester);
Bottom left: Jill (Miss Brighton);
Bottom right: June Pooley (Miss Hove)
in the centre Film Star Patrick Holt

Poster of Pantomime at the Grand Theatre 1947
Note Morecombe and Wise in early days – Jill just below

Cast on stage – Jack and the Beanstalk. Grand Theatre 1947. Jill in middle of three girls wearing long flowing dresses. Morecombe and Wise – long white 'stockings' – straw hats

Epilogue

The winter of 1948, was to be a lot less harsh than the unforgettable nightmare of 1947. Towards the end of February there was some extremely cold weather, but this was with mainly clear skies – there was little snow. The summer, could only be described, 'a typical English summer' – with the exception of the latter part of July, when there was a heat wave with temperatures soaring into the nineties, but these unusual tropical temperatures were short lived.

Further afield from Sussex and the home shores, in India, on January 30th 1948, Mahatma Gandhi was assassinated – a martyr, perhaps a saint! One of the newspaper reports said – "Mahatma Gandhi, the man who, more than any other secured India's freedom from British rule, was assassinated by one of his own countrymen in New Delhi today. The next day brought unforgettable scenes on the banks of The Jumna river as his body was cremated and his ashes cast on to the river."

On May 14th 1948, a report from Palestine said: "At 4pm today – eight hours before the British mandate in Palestine was due to end, the Jews proclaimed the new state of Israel. David Ben-Gurion, the Jewish Agency leader, is to be Prime Minister of a provisional government until a general election is held in October. Most vehicles in Tel-Aviv are now sporting the new blue and white Israeli flag – two horizontal bars and a star of David.

In Hastings 'PM' lives in very different circumstances to those in 1947, her front garden attractively planted out with many varieties of flowers – a 'cosy nest.'

189

At Wepham, Audrey and Jack O'Neill have a view from their beautiful home deep in the Sussex countryside, which looks towards Arundel Castle – three miles or so away as the crow flies – it is a view to savour. They are both well and enjoy the serenity of this quiet corner of the county.

Gerald Summers spent quite a few years in Africa. Back in this country he married his wife Imogen in 1967, and after this, with a lot of support from his wife and others – the writing began. Now, several memorable and highly enjoyable books later, he still lives in Wales – "but Sussex is always on my mind," he told me recently, "I love it above all other places!"

At Lancing College, at the beginning of the centenary celebrations, on July 23rd 1948 – the sanatorium became the boarding place for girls from some of the other Woodard schools, and a special camp was set up to accommodate boys from various other ones.

A special marquee had been put up about two weeks before this for the photographers from 'Picture Post' to display their photographs. They had been busily covering various activities going on in the school, in the run up to the centenary celebrations. One of these, was of a house party held by Mr. Chamberlin in Teme House. In the copy of Picture Post, dated July 17th 1948, the article accompanying the photographs, which takes up five pages of this famous old magazine, was written by Basil Handford – 'Mr. Chips'- as he later became known, he was master for a long time at Lancing, including the time I was there. He has also written a book which is the history of Lancing College, and is simply called – 'Lancing College.' A more recent book by Jeremy Tomlinson, is called, 'Lancing College – A Portrait.'

Basil Handford ends his article in The Picture Post, as follows:
"It will be a great day for Lancing on July 24th, when Lord Halifax and other distinguished guests, 17 bishops, representatives of the other Woodard schools, old boys and parents gather

190

together in this great chapel to give thanks for the completion of one hundred years of school life, and to hear the new cantata, St. Nicolas, which Benjamin Britten has specially composed to do honour to the college of St. Mary and Nicolas, Lancing."

Father and Sylvia with my great-aunt May attended the celebrations at Lancing that day – father preferred not to go to the cantata, as his leg wouldn't take having to sit for so long in the packed chapel; I spent that time showing him around parts of the school he hadn't seen before. Sylvia and Aunt May thoroughly enjoyed the music. Aunt May, now had a grandson – my cousin Jonathan – and a great nephew at the college; her husband, Lance Knowles, who had died in 1943, was secretary of Sussex County Cricket Club for twenty two years, and had played for both Kent and Sussex as an amateur.

The pantomime at The Grand Theatre did very well. After this Jill went on to do further modelling jobs before marrying Johnnie Silverside -a top photographer on the News Chronicle. Sadly, Johnnie passed away in 1996 – they had had a long and happy marriage together, during which, he saw Jill win an Emmy award with Jane Robinson for their designs for the Thames T.V production of 'Jenny,' Lady Randolph Churchill.

My father died in 1959. Sylvia is still alive and well and lives in Oxford, she is a nonagenarian and much loved member of the family.

I saw John and Rita Brown on a recent trip to Barcombe Mills – they are both well. They no longer hire out boats or serve teas; at this stage in their lives they are content with the quieter life in their corner of Sussex, where the river and its wildlife is much as I remember it – just beautiful!

The Author

David Knowles lives with his wife in Rochester.
As a writer and very small publisher, he is interested in helping to bring to light any worthwhile true stories of the twentieth century – "Before they are forgotten."

The author introducing grand-daughter Kerry to the quiet waters of a branch of the Sussex Ouse at Barcombe Mills – summer 1999.